Service 101

It's Time to Understand Customer Service

Published by: John L. Bustard
2015

First Printing: 2015

ISBN-13: 978-1511962667

Published by: John L. Bustard
Email: jlb27@outlook.com

Contents

Welcome

To the world of customer service.

The primary audience for this book is students and professionals that do not understand the world of customer service.

You have probably taken courses in liberal arts, engineering, business management, or the sciences, but unfortunately there are few courses, if any, on the important topic of customer service.

If you are a student, customer service can be a whole career of its own and my intent is to introduce you to that world.

If you are already employed, maybe you have or are developing products for the marketplace and you need to make sure you are prepared to support them. Like many people, you are not sure what you will need to accomplish or who you will need to engage to define and then execute a service support plan.

Others of you have already introduced products to the marketplace but product acceptance is less than stellar, partly because of your customer's service experience. I will make sure you know what it means to provide great customer service.

If you are in sales, marketing, or product development, you will not have success without good customer service. That success will depend on you partnering with your customer service team and better understanding their daily tasks and challenges.

This book is to allow you to learn. We will start by addressing a "service plan", i.e. how a company plans to provide its customers service. You will immediately see there is a lot to it.

This book has been written with the premise that you the reader are now in a job where you must decide how you will setup customer service for your company's products. What do you need to know, what options do you have, and what decisions will you need to make.

Enjoy the journey. I spent a whole career at it.

Service Plan

The service plan is explained in a document that summarizes all of the key aspects regarding your products, and how you will support them. Being concise but complete are keys to success, so everyone on your team knows the total picture and their role in it. Each item in the plan will then need to have details spelled out for which we will help you understand what is required in this book.

Customer expectations and how you want to be positioned in the marketplace drive your service strategy which then drives your service plan. We are going to start with a sample service plan so you better understand everything involved in providing great customer service.

Below is an example service plan for product family xyz. As you develop your plan, there can be multiple different options for many of the service functions. You and your team will need to define which is correct for you. We will help you understand the options.

Example Service Plan

Product family xyz – is a major capital purchase for our customers, requires ongoing consumables which can only be purchased through us. When service is required, we estimate that 25% of the time the customer can solve the issue themselves, 50% of the time we can assist the customer and solve the issue remotely, but 25% of the time will require on-site service by a person trained in servicing our product.

Customer operation – 24x7, downtime directly impacts customer profitability, as well as ours, since downtime means the customer is not using our consumables

Geographies – we market and sell globally in 35 countries.

Service strategy – our product family is a premium product in the marketplace for which we need to provide premium service. We use service to ensure product uptime to drive profitable consumable sales. Our customers expect and we will deliver a consistent customer experience globally. We will differentiate ourselves through our people and partner personnel focused on quality service supported by a robust remote services capability and high service part availability. We want industry standard margins for service and consumables in combination.

Sales and service channels – we will have direct sales and service in the United States, Canada, and Western Europe. Dealer sales and service in Asia, Latin America, Eastern Europe and the Middle East

Direct service pricing – preferred pricing is for service and consumables to be bundled and sold as a cost/widget. Optionally the customer can purchase consumables and service separately, with service sold as a service agreement, or on an ala carte time & material basis. Billing is generally monthly. Service agreements are "evergreen" meaning 60 days advance notice is required by the customer to terminate the service agreement.

Direct services available - installation & start-up services, educational services, professional services, and repair & maintenance services

Repair & maintenance service levels – standard pricing is for standard business hours with a response time goal of next business day if on-site service is required. Expedited and extended hours coverage options exist, such as 24x7 with 4 hour response on-site, for a % uplift.

Dealer services & pricing – knowledge access, training classes, and service parts are all fee based. Dealers can also have us provide remote support on their behalf for a fee.

Knowledge – technical knowledge is available through multiple channels for those with advance entitlement. Our product has a knowledge widget embedded within our product software that accesses our knowledgebase via the web. Access to knowledge is also supported via the web through html5 enabled devices (smartphones, tablets, and PCs)

Remote service – our products connect via the web to our remote management capability which remotely monitors product health and proactively initiates service, when required. Our remote service centers in the U.S., Germany, and China will provide "follow-the-sun" support.

Web self-service – in addition to our remote management monitoring, customers can request service and monitor our service response through a product widget or directly via the web (smartphone, tablet, PC)

Service request workflow – we will first confirm customer service entitlement for the service requested based on service coverage purchased. Remote engineers will attempt remote diagnosis and fix. If on-site service is required, the remote engineers will order service parts, if known, and arrange for on-site service to be performed. Standard call status (e.g. enroute, on-site, complete, incomplete), and call closure information (e.g. issue, resolution, parts used) will be recorded and available in service history and to determine call billing

Resource staffing – remote engineering staffing will be able to respond to 90% of service incidents within 1 hour of creation of the service incident during the hours of coverage purchased by the customer. On-site service technicians will be on-site 90% of the time within the response time objective purchased by the customer.

On-site technician training – due to the complexity and uniqueness of our product, 3 weeks of training is required. One week can be interactive via the web, but the second and third week needs to be hands-on at one of our regional training centers

Service tools – proprietary diagnostics will reside on our servers to assist in the diagnosis of incident issues. Access to these entitled diagnostic algorithms will be entitled based. All tools required by on-site service technicians are industry standard service tools and no special tools will be required.

Service part pricing – list price will be 8x manufacturing cost for parts unique to our product. Industry standard parts will have a mark-up sufficient to cover inventory, handling, and reasonable margin, recognizing we prefer to have the dealers buy from us than alternative sources.

Service parts logistics network – lower priced "wearable" parts will be stocked locally by on-site personnel. "Random" failure parts and higher priced "wearable" parts will be stocked to allow next day delivery.

Service part sourcing – initially all service parts will be purchased new and deployed with the objective that 95% of service calls can be fixed through next day service. Expensive parts will be analyzed to determine whether repair options exist. Later in the product's life cycle strip/salvage will be utilized to reduce "all time buy" requirements.

Service part returns – all service parts will be returned for environmental disposition or repair.

Customer satisfaction – transaction based surveys will be used to measure customer satisfaction with service performed. Local service leadership will follow-up with every customer that submits an unsatisfactory survey response.

Key service metrics – we will monitor our business on the following key metrics

- **Customer satisfaction** – from incident transaction based surveys
- **Profitability** – margin and % margin for service and consumables combined
- **Customer profitability** - % of customers and % of customer value which is profitable for service and consumables combined
- **Service agreement coverage** - % of customers and service revenue with service agreements instead of time & material service
- **Response goal met** - % of remote support and % of on-site support that meet response time goals
- **First trip complete** - % of incidents resolved by remote, % resolved by 1 trip to customer site, % requiring additional support
- **Inventory investment $** - as a percent of service revenue

Service processes and systems – there are no unique requirements for product xyz. Our current service processes and systems suffice.

The sample service plan for product family xyz is concise, but at the same time covers all topics required for effective service.

Bet you had no idea just how much is involved in providing service for your company's products. The example service plan is an excellent summary of how we will provide service for product family xyz.

As I indicated earlier, there were other alternatives, and to allow you to better understand the options available to you, let's first describe the key functions found in any well operating service environment.

As we discuss this, remember that each function can be done by your organization, an outsource partner, a channel partner such as a dealer, or even the customer themselves. The important point is someone needs to address and decide the approach for each function that provides your customer a good service experience. That is you.

Service Environment

For service the customer is the center of the universe. To effectively service the customer, your product may require capabilities in each or some of the following:

- Incident management
- Knowledge management
- Remote service
- Depot service
- On-site service
- Service parts
- Service engineering
- Analytics & business management
- Contract administration

Definitions

The customer – the person that uses or operates your product. This can be different than the person to whom you sold the product. In the consumer space, your product may have been a gift. In the commercial space it is normal for the person that purchased the product to be different than the operator of the product.

Incident management – the end to end process that manages a service request, or what we call a service incident until service is complete. This will include logging the service request, verifying entitlement for service, assigning resources to provide service, ensuring service is performed, escalating if it is not, documenting the service provided, determining whether billing is required for services rendered, and initiating billing and invoicing, if appropriate.

Knowledge management – the personnel that provide service, (including potentially the customer through self-service) will require knowledge and training on how to provide the necessary service. This information typically resides in an entitled knowledgebase. There is a knowledge workflow that manages the process of knowledge creation, knowledge certification, knowledge publication, and even knowledge translation into multiple languages. There is knowledge meta data required to facilitate search and hierarchical presentation. There is also a role that defines access rights, i.e. person x is entitled to access knowledge y. This all encompasses knowledge management.

Remote service – service that can be performed on your product from a remote site. There are typically four different types of remote services possible, which are a function of your product design. These are:

- **Self-updating** – your company automatically downloads updates to your product on a periodic basis
- **Dial home** – your product has a built in feature, which automatically contacts your remote service capability when it encounters an issue. At this time it can automatically initiate programmatic diagnostic routines and even perform self-updates based on your diagnostic logic, or your remote service engineers can be engaged and provide human assistance.
- **Call out** – your product allows the remote service engineers to remotely access your product in a call out mode, but the

product cannot call home. In this scenario, the customer must typically contact you to request service.

- **Telephone or chat support** – your product or customer does not allow you to have access to your product through the network. Your remote service engineers can talk or chat with the customer to provide instructions on what steps to take to diagnose and fix the service situation.

Depot service – your product is sent to a depot where service is performed. There are typically two types of depot service that can be visible to your customers

- **Return for repair** – the customer ships the product to your designated repair facility, where it is repaired or periodic maintenance is performed and then returned to the customer.
- **Advanced unit replacement** – you ship the customer a new or reconditioned unit, and they ship you back (typically in the same box) the non-working unit. The customer does not expect back the non-working unit, which you can repair/recondition and add to a pool for the next customer that needs an advanced unit replacement.

On-site service – a service technician is dispatched to the product site to perform service.

Service parts – effective service requires access to service parts. A common phrase in the service industry is "we need the right part at the right place at the right time". To achieve this for a product that will be serviced globally requires

- **Part planning & procurement** – define sources of supply, enter contracts, negotiate pricing, forecast demand, place

orders, address backorders and quality issues, deploy available inventory to global stocking locations
- **Warehousing** – management of stocking locations globally that will allow timely delivery of service parts to service providers within the terms sold to your customers.
- **Transportation** – delivery of service parts to service providers is typically in one of three ways
  - Expedited same day delivery
  - Next day delivery
  - Replenishment delivery – 2 or more days
- **Return logistics** – the process of returning parts from the point of service. There are typically three possibilities
  - Return unused parts to inventory – in anticipation of the service situation, parts 1, 2, and 3 were sent to the customer site, but only part 1 and 2 were required to resolve the service incident. In this case part 3 can be returned to inventory.
  - Return for environmental disposition – meta data about the service part indicates there is special processing required for its disposal
  - Return for repair/reconditioning – typically an expensive part, such as a circuit board or an assembly, for which it is too difficult to diagnose or repair at the customer site, but which can be repaired at a depot.
- **Strip/salvage** – every product has a life cycle. At product introduction, service parts are typically new. Later in the product's life, a strip/salvage of used product for service parts is a very viable source of service parts.

Service Engineering – the product technical experts that specialize in service. Typically there are five key tasks

- **Serviceability** – ensuring during product design that the product can be effectively serviced
- **Service parts** – identifying which parts will be service parts, estimating reliability for use in service part forecasting models
- **Knowledge & training** – the subject matter expert that defines how the product is to be diagnosed and what the repair procedure will be. Certifies documentation and training materials developed
- **Higher level technical support** – if the response center engineers or the on-site service technicians cannot resolve the service situation it gets escalated to the service engineer typically before going to product development. The service engineer may need to fly on-site to provide assistance.
- **Corrective action** – based on all service incidents, what corrective action is required to the product or as input to the next generation of the product to improve service performance. What corrective action is required of our training programs to improve operational performance? Are their specific response engineers or on-site service technicians that need additional training?

Contract administration – typically companies do not provide free service to anyone that wants it. The customer is entitled to various levels of service based on whether they are on warranty, or what type of service agreement they purchased, or whether they are time & material (pay for each service incident separately). Contract administration can consist of the following functions (unless performed elsewhere in the organization)

15

- **Quoting** – estimating the price of service to allow it to be sold and then packaging it as an offer/quote to the customer for their acceptance
- **Invoicing** – once an offer/quote has been accepted by the customer, it must be billed and invoiced according to the terms agreed to with the customer, typically annually, quarterly, or monthly
- **Revenue recognition** – special accounting rules apply to recognizing service revenue in a company's P&L. For example if a $1200 service contract runs from July 1st through June 30 of the next year, then revenue needs to be recognized as $100/month or $600 this year and $600 next year.
- **Installed base & entitlement data** – this can have different levels of detail depending on the product. It can be simply a list of product serial #s that are entitled to warranty service without regard to who requests service, or it could be a full set of information such as customer name, address, product installed, software version, service contract sold, etc.

Congratulations, you have now seen a sample service plan and understand the service functions necessary to execute that service plan. You ca n also see that each function listed can be a career itself.

Now we want to assume you have been asked to setup a service organization for your company. You now have to make choices on how you will deliver service to your customers. There are many options – more than you might think. We will discuss them in greater detail. This will allow you to develop a service plan for your company.

Before we start, if you are a student, it's time to think of a product for which you will need to develop a service plan. There are many options. It could be a smart phone, or a TV, a computer, an automobile, enterprise software, an elevator, a large earth moving piece of equipment, etc. As you can envision, everything we use in our daily life, either at business or for our personal use, can require service and therefore there will need to be a service plan. If you already work for a company, which of its products will you use as your product family for your service plan?

As we go through the details for each service area, think about what option is best for the product you chose.

How You Want to Position Service in the Marketplace

Let's start by using an example from the past to better understand this: How two different companies could have positioned compact digital cameras and their service in the marketplace.

Both companies were well aware that smart phones would replace the need for low end compact digital cameras within a few years, but there was still an opportunity to make money now.

- **Company A** - was known for its high end digital cameras. It also sold compact digital cameras, and hoped that those customers would graduate to their higher end cameras. It was therefore important that a customer with a service issue have a great service experience. Whenever a customer contacted them with a service issue by phone, they extended the call by making sure they answered any questions the customer had regarding getting great photos. They also developed training materials and periodic emails on how to get great photos. In short they built their service strategy to facilitate a long term relationship with the customer and provide an upgrade path to higher value cameras.
- **Company B** – was transitioning themselves away from photography, but saw the compact digital camera market as an opportunity to generate cash for investment in their future elsewhere. They wanted to sell volume, including "Black Friday" front page ad "deals". They determined that

customers decided their camera model & brand based on price and features, and not on service. They built their service strategy to minimize service cost, recognizing they did not have a long term relationship with the customer anyway.

As you can envision, the documented service plans for company A and B will be quite different.

Just consider telephone support. Company B's strategy implies longer hold times to customer service, greater focus on lowering the call duration of providing support, and greater use of lower cost off shore agents than we would find for company A.

Remember, how service is delivered is determined through the service strategy which must be in alignment with the overall market strategy for your product. This will differ from company to company depending on how they want to position themselves in the marketplace.

Customer Expectations

Before you decide how you want to position yourself competitively, you need to make sure you understand customer expectations and decide which of those expectations you want to meet. This can differ drastically by product, market, and geography.

Let's give an example again dealing with compact digital cameras.

In the U.S., customers expected to be able to contact the manufacturer and receive service directly. This makes market sense since compact digital cameras were primarily sold through mass retailers. To be cost competitive, the manufacturer focused on web self-service supplemented by telephone and chat support. If the camera required repair or replacement, the repair transaction was for a single camera for a single customer.

Europe sold more of their compact digital cameras through specialty shops. The customers expected to get answers from the store and if the camera needed replacement or repair have it processed through the store. This required different system support. There was a greater focus on educating store personnel about camera operation and issues, and allowing a store to return multiple cameras in a single repair transaction.

You need to make sure you are in tune with the cultural and geographic differences globally as you build your plan.

Many times within a company there is an assumption that how we supported a previous product is how we will service the next generation. The company can easily develop inertia regarding improvements to the processes and systems to stay current.

Advances in technology can also raise customer expectations beyond your current ability to meet them with your legacy organizational structures, processes and systems. In this case leadership has some difficult organizational and investment decisions. This can become obvious to leadership as a result of new product based on newer technology, or can be generic to all products of your portfolio.

Let me give an example.

In the commercial product space many companies historically organized service by geography, i.e. the U.S. & Canada, Latin America, Europe, Asia, the Middle East or various combinations of these.

Each geography developed their own processes and supporting service systems unique to their geography.

These were significant legacy investments and well entrenched organizationally.

Some companies even operate with multiple totally independent divisions, so even in a region such as Europe there could be multiple processes and systems since each division had a separate solution.

The CEO visited key global customers to hear the same thing:

- We want one set of service terms globally
- We want a common global process that is web enabled for requesting service

- We want to monitor your service response consistently across all global sites.
- If we need to operate differently by product and region, then why do we need you?

This is a broader issue than the service plan tied to a new product introduction and raises the question of when does leadership need to re-engineer the company based on changing customer expectations across our total product portfolio.

Service Plan Details

It's now time to address each component of your service plan in greater detail. Here we will make sure you are adequately educated to make intelligent decisions.

The Customer

Everything starts and revolves around the customer. You need to understand their objectives, their business model, and their environment in detail.

Consider the manufacturer of large earth moving equipment, e.g. used in the construction of highways globally. The equipment will operate in the extreme cold (e.g. northern Alaska), in desserts, in high tropics (e.g. the Amazon), in high altitudes, etc. Each of these environments will have an impact on product reliability as well as impact ease of repair. As one example, the price of a "standard service agreement" targeted for normal use in a normal climate will probably be totally inadequate when the product is used in more extreme weather situations, even though they are normal for that geographic area.

Assume our product is a high end printer. The customer that demands high quality color output will have greater service demands than the person printing monthly credit card invoices.

Where the product operates, even in an office environment, can impact service demand. We previously introduced an office based product to the marketplace to find our failure rates were much higher than anticipated, with some customers operating fine and others having excessive failure. It took months before a SWAT team determined the cause. Some geographies had more thunderstorms than others, sending electrical surges through our product electronics. We fixed this through a product modification.

Many banks operate standard business hours and may include Saturday and Sunday hours, but usually during the day. Retail, on the other hand, especially grocery stores can be open 24x7. If your product supports the checkout lanes, and you need to install an upgrade, when will you be asked to do it? Probably in the lower volume time, ala the middle of the night.

There are many different types of product and many different types of customers, so your list of questions needs to be customized to your situation. Here are some areas to consider:

Customer audience – who uses your product. This will have a huge impact on your service plan. For example is your audience a set of engineers or does it include multiple generations, such as grandparents, parents, and children, all with different levels of technical skills.

Global – where will your product be sold? Can everyone read English? How many languages will you need to support?

Environment – what are the environmental specifications for our product? Will the customer being using the product within these specifications?

Quality – what tolerance will our customer have regarding quality output? For example, printing a newspaper will have a lot higher tolerance on image quality than printing wedding photos

Operators – if our product requires operators, what level of turnover is there, who handles training, what is the incremental cost to us if our customer's operators are not adequately trained. What is the impact on the B&C shifts if those operators are less trained and proficient than the A shift operator(s)?

Price – for each "widget" produced in conjunction with our product, how much revenue does the customer receive? What portion of that can be our revenue?

Consumables – will the customer purchase the consumables from a third party? Does a third party consumable impact how much service is required on our product?

Seasonality – are there seasons, such as Christmas, that will have greater service demand than other seasons? How will this impact our staffing and overtime?

Criticality – when service is required, how fast is it required? If on-site is required, can it wait until tomorrow (if it must be today, then there is an impact on parts stocking and locally trained on-site service technicians). What are the response time and hours of coverage requirements? Do we have significant placement density to support local trained on-site resources?

Service Offerings and Contracts

I have met a lot of people that when they think of the word "product", they think of something physical: a TV, a smartphone, an automobile. All of these and many more are "products". A company that makes products must decide what versions they will sell and what they will pass on and either not offer to the marketplace or exit from what they previously offered.

Service is also a product, and a company must decide how they will package their service products into product offerings.

Typically physical products are sold with a warranty. The warranty is a service product which is bundled with the sale of the physical product itself. Just like all other products, it comes with a set of terms and conditions.

The terms specify what is included under warranty and what is not. An automobile is a good example, where we find that oil changes and tire replacement are not typically included in the warranty. For smartphones, product failure is included, but if you drop the smartphone it is not covered.

Companies will provide enhancement options, e.g. extended warranties. This could extend the warranty to a second or third year, or include coverage for a "dropped smartphone".

I live in western New York, where we are known to get a lot of snow. Sometimes we will lose our electricity. My wife and I purchased and had installed a gas generator that will come on automatically on loss of electricity. The installation of the product required an electrician. He performed what the industry calls "installation services". Installation services can be bundled in the price of the product, sold as a separate flat fee service, or sold on an hourly or quoted basis. Those are decisions you need to make about your product. There is not one correct answer.

At work we purchased an enterprise software package that needed to be configured for our operation and connected with other software used by our company. We utilized experts from the software provider, who charged us "professional services" fees to assist us in implementing their software. "Professional services" is another example of a service product.

Let's assume we have a major capital product that we purchased and for which we had installation services to install the product, and professional services to help us integrate it into our workflow. It is time to train our operators on how to effectively use the product. In the service industry, we call that "educational services". Once again, the fee for educational services can be bundled into the price of the product itself or sold separately. Again, that is your choice.

Not all products are sold with a warranty, and even when they are, at some point the warranty will expire. At the end of the warranty, companies will allow a customer to purchase a "service agreement" or they can obtain service on a "time & material" basis.

A service agreement can be beneficial to both the customer and the service provider.

For the customer, it typically provides "peace of mind", in that it is a fixed fee that can be budgeted. Many times service providers give preferential service to their service agreement customers. We all worry about that catastrophic failure in a product we purchased that will cost us a fortune. With a service agreement, we are purchasing an insurance policy in conjunction with everyone else that purchased a service agreement.

For the service provider, a service agreement represents known revenue. It also allows a company to know where their service volume will be geographically, and therefore can justify training of resources, and stocking of service parts.

One service agreement product does not fit all customers. Through your customer analysis (discussed earlier), you must identify what options to offer. Two common options deal with response time and hours of coverage.

Customers that do not purchase a service agreement receive service on a "time & material" basis. Typically there is an hourly rate for travel and service hours and all parts are charged at list price.

Let's assume we have a customer who purchased a service agreement which calls for 24x7 on-site service. As the service provider we have to have our service technician on call to respond. That's not free. Typically our service technician is paid for the hours they work (normal hours or called out hours) as well as they receive a $ amount for being on-call, meaning they are prepared to interrupt whatever they are doing in their personal life to respond to the customer.

This is why companies do not offer time & material customers the option for after-hours service. When a customer is time & material there is no contractual agreement between the parties.

The service provider may get asked to provide service or the customer may ask someone else. Why would the service provider pay to have someone on call, when they may never get called?

Likewise, the service provider will not want to invest in a local set of parts if they don't know if they will ever be needed. Therefore, typically time & material customers get what we call lower levels of service and rightfully so.

Now it's almost time for you to decide what service products you will offer the marketplace. First a few more key points.

If a product is not selling well in the marketplace, a company can always withdraw it, and no longer sell it. That is not true for a service product. A company can also discontinue the sale of newly effective service agreements, but must honor any outstanding warranty or already sold service agreements to whatever termination clauses were included in those contracts. This could obligate the company for multiple years.

In many cases, warranties or service agreements expire after a year, so you may think a company can exit a losing product within a year. Again, not so. Customers must be offered time & material service for a legally specified time period which differs by country and is generally tied to the date of last sale of the product in the marketplace. This can get quite interesting. If you sell consumer products through channel partners and even though you no longer ship product to your dealers, you have to take into account how long it takes them to clear their inventory in determining your service discontinuance date.

Many companies are finding that their global customers expect consistency globally. The definition of a full service contract in the U.S. needs to be the same as the definition in Asia, Europe, etc. I can guarantee you, especially if historically you have operated as independent regions globally, that your people will not believe you can have a common set of service terms globally. In our case it took 6 months of a global team's effort to realize that 95%+ of our service revenues could be defined in a finite set of common terms.

The breakthrough was in what terminology we used. In the U.S. the standard business days for an office environment are Monday through Friday, but in Israel it is Sunday through Thursday. In the U.S. our standard business hours are 8:00 am to 5:00 pm, but in other countries it is 8:30 to 5:00, or 9:00 to 6:00, or 9:00 to 6:30, etc.

Of course, no one thought we could have a common set of terms since they all were thinking in terms of 8:00 – 5:00, etc. We changed and started to use terminology such as "standard business hours", "newspaper hours", "2 shift", "24x7", and quickly we found a lot of commonality.

I led a team to globalize service processes and systems for a major global company that utilized SAP as its core enterprise software. A high priced SAP guru gave me some very good advice. He said you can define all of your terms for one country and then define them again for the second country you implement, etc., but you will die in administration. Define what is common globally and then define exceptions for what is not. This is very significant, since it means you need to have a global view upfront, which may be totally inconsistent with how you operate today.

There is another key learning we had with this initiative. I had someone tell me that everyone knows what a full service contract represents. My response was everybody except the computer and they need to know going forward. In the past, a person used the telephone to request service to another person. That person on our behalf knew what a full service contract was, and could take action to ensure service was performed accordingly. Now the customer pushes a widget on their product, or requests service through the web, and there is no human that represents our company. Our terms not only need to be consistent globally, but the computer must be able to programmatically understand them and take appropriate action.

Service Pricing

Service pricing is a very interesting topic, because it can be done in so many ways. Once again, you have decisions to make.

Historically, in one approach to pricing, a service agreement would have a price. You and the customer may negotiate on that price and agree to a discount, if appropriate. This would be the price of the service agreement based on its terms and conditions. Service performed outside the service agreement terms and conditions would be charged at time & material rates.

Historically, in a second approach to pricing, service would be quoted as a percent of the sale price of the product to be serviced. If service was quoted at 10%, and the product sold for $100k, then the service price would be $10k. If the customer negotiated a 10% discount on the product sale to $90k, then the service price would be $9k. Once again service performed outside the service agreement terms and conditions would be charged at time & material rates.

Historically, a third alternative was bundled pricing, which may include the product itself, the consumables, and service all for a fee/widget produced. And yes, service outside whatever the terms and conditions of service would be charged at time & material rates.

I have heard of companies approaching it entirely differently. Their premise is they would prefer that the customer be on a service agreement rather than time & material, as long as they can make an adequate margin. They are using analytic data on their service experience with the customer to decide what to quote. Their view is the customer maybe using the product out of spec, they may not have their operators trained as required; all of that is ok as long as we can price taking that into account.

Before you decide how to do your pricing, there are two other things you should be aware of.

First, most companies use purchased software, such as SAP, or another enterprise software package. The software company defines their pricing capability as an industry best practice – it is really what their software supports. Your contract administrators will be much more productive if your pricing approach subscribes to how your software operates and very unproductive if it doesn't. And this is very difficult to get across to your marketing teams and senior leadership.

Second, beware of fair market pricing laws.

At this time, you should know what you want your service products to be and how you will price them. We now need to better understand each component of providing service, and therefore whether you will have profitable customer service.

Self-Service

Self-service is where the customer resolves their issue without engaging the service provider, such as the manufacturer.

The classic example of this is the grandparents that call their children or grandchildren to find the answer to their issue. Their children or grandchildren, being more technically inclined, may know the answer, or may search for the answer on the grandparent's behalf.

Self-service is not free to the service provider, it is just much less expensive from an operational standpoint than any other alternative.

Self-service can and will require an investment by the service provider. There are three specific types of investment and ongoing costs that can be incurred by the service provider

- **Web self-service environment** – typically a web environment that contains knowledge and/or diagnostics that can be searched and accessed by customers to get the appropriate information to allow them to resolve the issue themselves. If programmatic diagnostics are included, then they may also be able to self-correct the situation. In this situation, the web environment, the knowledge itself, the diagnostics, and the self-correcting routines all represent investments by the service provider.
- **The product itself** – an upfront investment can allow the product itself to self-correct itself with the assistance of the customer.
- **Community support** – the service provider can establish a community environment where customers can assist each

other in an environment managed by the service provider. There are three specific areas to consider:

- **Recognition** – the community members that provide support are recognized
- **Support oversight** – if the community provides incorrect solutions, or a person posts negative and incorrect information about your product, then the service provider must intercede.
- **No one provides an answer** – if no one from the community answers a post within x hours, the service provider needs to jump in and provide an answer.
- The key point about community support is the community addresses x% of the issues at little cost to the service provider, but the service provider will still need to provide the environment, manage it, and address y% of the issues.

Self-service can either be encouraged or even mandated before getting higher level support, such as telephone or chat support. Some examples include:

- A service provider's service agreement with a national chain specifies that the retail location will contact a central location to attempt to resolve the issue before contacting the service provider. It can even be that only the central location can log the service request with the service provider.
- Telephone and chat support queues can provide lists of top issues that can be easily accessed by the customer
- An incident must be created on the web before contacting telephone or chat support. The incident must include a "problem description" which automatically searches for

known solutions and presents them to the customer as part of the incident logging process.

Incident Management

To understand core concepts, let's think about incident management as it actually existed 40 years ago. For many of you, this will seem "ancient" from a technology standpoint, but many of the concepts apply today.

- The local office had a large round table with a number of dispatchers and a lazy susan in the middle.
- The lazy susan had slots for each service technician, and could be spun so each of the dispatchers could access the slots for any one of the service technicians.
- There were actually three slots for each service technician, with the top slot being open incidents, the middle slot being those incidents communicated to the service technician, and the bottom slot being completed incidents.
- The customer called the local office to request service and talked with a dispatcher.
- The dispatcher recorded the service request as an incident on a colored index card. There was a different color for each day of the week.
- The dispatcher knew the geography, and therefore had knowledge to know to which service technician to assign the incident. The new service incident was put in the top slot for the service technician.
- If the service request was urgent, the dispatcher could page the service technician. Otherwise, the service technician called in periodically during the day.
- When the service technician called the dispatcher, if the incident was completed the index card was moved to the

bottom slot from the middle slot. New incidents were communicated to the service technician and moved from the top slot to the middle slot.

- At any time the dispatchers or leadership could spin the lazy susan and see the status of the local office. If one service technician had too many incidents, they could be reassigned to another. The color scheme allowed knowledge on whether incidents were being closed reasonably, e.g. if a Monday colored incident was still open on a Wednesday, that needed to be addressed.

The core concept of incident management as embedded in the lazy susan solution still applies today, i.e. a process to log and act on a service incident.

There have been a number of advantages of computerization. These include:

- Not dependent on "tribal knowledge" of individuals, e.g. the dispatcher knew that if the incident was from customer "A", it was to be assigned to service technician "B". Automated techniques allow for incident handling to be done in central locations and/or by the computer.
- Service terms such as hours of coverage and response time can differ from one customer to another and be appropriately handled.
- Products can "call home" and be programmatically logged and acted on.
- Customers can request service through the web and monitor the response through the web.

As you design your incident management environment, there are a number of decisions you will need to make. Let's discuss them:

Web logging – do your customers expect to and do you want your customers to have the ability to log service incidents through the web. Hopefully your answer is yes, but this creates a number of issues to resolve:

- **Simple** – the process must be simple, or the customer will not use it
- **Identification** – how do you want your customer to identify themselves, so you can autofill in many of the fields required for a service incident, such as name, street address, product to be serviced, service agreement coverage, etc. How will you manage the identification list?
- **Coverage type** – some companies will allow customers who purchased service agreements to log service incidents via the web, but require time & material customers to call them, given the greater complexity of the incident logging process (e.g. a credit check, getting a purchase order or credit card, providing a quote, etc.)
- **Secure** – it would be a disaster if your competition could spider your web logging capability and steal your installed base data. For example, if you only required your customer to provide a product serial #, then the competition can spider your site by requesting service for each possible serial #. When you auto-fill most fields, such as customer name, address, product name, etc., the competition has total access to your installed base of customers. You only want your customer to be able to see their data.

Incident handling team – even if customers can request service via the web or a product widget, some will still want to call. Plus there must be an organization that does oversight on all incidents and addresses any exception processing required.

Internal or outsourced resources

We found higher customer satisfaction and lower total cost when we managed ourselves a core set of internal resources supplemented by contract resources instead of utilizing an outsource provider.

The primary reason was customer and product knowledge required and much lower turnover. Our products were complex.

Languages – how many different languages does your incident handling team need to support on a global basis. North and South America will require English, French, Spanish, and Portuguese. Europe will require at a minimum English, French, German, Spanish, Italian, and Portuguese, plus potentially Russian. Asia will require English, Chinese, Japanese, and Korean, and potentially others.

Hours of coverage – what days and hours of coverage are required by geography and product family

Follow the sun – what sites and language combinations will allow required coverage, potentially 24x7

Staffing – for customers that contact you by telephone or chat, what amount of hold time is acceptable? You will need to know the statistical distribution of incoming calls, and what is the distribution of call duration. This will allow you to determine the staffing levels required.

Incident/knowledge integration

Historically the knowledge system was standalone and independent of the incident management system. Those days should be in the past.

When you or the customer enter an issue into the incident it should automatically search the knowledgebase. These should be integrated solutions.

Whose system

If you use an outsource provider for your incident handling team, they will tell you it is best to utilize their system for which you then don't need to invest. There are pro's and con's to this:

Your customers will expect to come to your web site, so you will need to integrate your supplier's incident management/knowledge solution with your web site

Your outsource provider potentially lowers your system investment cost, but makes it more difficult to change to a different supplier.

Queue design

Once an incident is logged to the system, what are the rules that define what queue it will be assigned for follow-up? Options include product family, type of customer issue, geography, and/or language.

Customer satisfaction surveys

The incident management system should have the ability to generate a transactional customer satisfaction survey at the completion of the incident based on a set of rules (e.g. do not survey a customer if they were recently surveyed). The survey response should be tied to the incident

If a customer provides an unsatisfactory survey response, we found that local supervision needed to first look into what happened on the incident, and then contact the customer to verbally discuss our service response. This requirement of local supervision increased our service performance and customer satisfaction.

In summary – incident management is a career in itself, either as the person who processes each incident, as a person who defines the process used in incident management, the software company that provides incident management toolsets, or the telecom company that provides the telecommunications infrastructure.

Knowledge Management

Tribal knowledge – all of us within our "brains" have what we will call tribal knowledge. If 1000's of customers request support and many of them have the same issue, then those that provide that support will quickly "know the answer". That is tribal knowledge.

Knowledgebase – this is where you want the solutions to the issues surfaced by your customers. You want them documented in your knowledgebase so anyone providing customer support can access the most up to date solution. The knowledgebase can also support self-service.

Your turn - a key challenge many companies face is getting tribal knowledge into their knowledgebase. The reason is simple – knowledge is powerful. If I know something you don't know then I am more important to the organization and less likely to be downsized or replaced. For your company, how will you overcome this? The industry calls this "change management", and we will discuss that as its own topic later in this book.

Timing – your response center or on-site personnel are "on point" with your customer.

They have an issue they must resolve.

If they find something that works it needs to be shared so other response center or on-site personnel that encounter the same issue (and a new issue can quickly become a high volume issue) know what one person did to resolve the issue.

This means the workflow for posting knowledge to the knowledgebase needs to be very fast, even if you indicate the solution as uncertified.

If you don't allow quick posting, you will find post-it notes or a secondary knowledgebase will develop, since your people "on point" with the customer will find a way to share what they know.

More "modern" incident management systems will allow the response center and on-site personnel to search incidents to see what solution was used. This is even faster than getting the solution into the knowledgebase.

Certification – timing and certification are in conflict. In some organizations the engineering organization will want to certify the solution before it is posted to the knowledgebase. There are different alternatives.

We found that we needed to post internally (by the response center and on-site personnel) immediately as uncertified knowledge, but then require certification before we would post the knowledge externally. There are two additional reasons for this:

- Sensitive knowledge – there are some issues and solutions that cannot be posted externally.
- Audience – how knowledge is written and understood by people that use it every day can be different than a customer that accesses it once. It may need to be re-written to be effective with the customer (see below).

Some companies post all non-sensitive knowledge immediately to the knowledgebase, including to external audiences, and mark it "uncertified".

This is a choice you need to make.

Writing to the audience – timing and writing to the audience are also in conflict, and you typically have multiple audiences

Response center and on-site personnel - will encounter the same issue over and over. When a new issue surfaces, getting it available in the knowledgebase quickly is critical, or each of your support personnel will need to figure out a solution that someone else already knows. These people also have greater technical knowledge on your product than you can expect of your customer. It is totally reasonable that a response center or on-site person quickly document what they did to resolve the issue and it is posted to the knowledgebase for internal use.

Customer – hopefully your customer will only encounter a situation once, and generally they will not have the same technical knowledge about your product.

In most cases this means the issue and solution will need to be rewritten before it is posted externally. Let me give a real-life example.

On Windows 7 or an earlier version there is a "system tray" in the bottom right of the screen. We had a knowledgebase solution that indicated go to the system tray and do x.

It was reasonable to assume that the response center and on-site personnel knew the concept of a Windows system tray, but we quickly learned that grandma and grandpa, who were key audiences of our product, had no understanding of the words "system tray".

We had no luck with self-service until we re-wrote the issue and solution in a way our customer understood, which included grandma and grandpa.

Meta data

Meta data is data about something. In the case of a product sold through retail, meta data will include the dimensions and weight of the box in which the product is sold.

For knowledge, meta data describes the knowledge. Let's give some examples:

- **Language** – the knowledge article is written in language x
- **Type of knowledge** – this knowledge article is an "issue/solution" document, or a "user manual", etc.
- **Product** – this knowledge article applies to product families' xyz.
- **Search** – a list of search terms the customer could use when searching for this knowledge article. It is important that this list be from the perspective of the person that will search for the document, and not from the perspective of the product engineer. We had a product for which the engineer titled the knowledge article as "image quality issues", but customers were searching using the phrase "no black" or "no color".
- **Navigation hierarchy** – studies have shown that younger generations tend to search for solutions and older generations navigate through a hierarchy. What node in the hierarchy does this knowledge article represent

- **Version** – for software, what software versions does this knowledge article apply to
- **Who and when** – who wrote the knowledge article, who certified it, and when.
- **Access rights** – who is allowed to view the knowledge, e.g. internal only vs. external

Appropriate meta data is critical to a knowledgebase success, particularly for self service.

Issue/resolution vs. reference data

When an organization has a lot of tribal knowledge, they find that their knowledgebase is primarily reference data. That is, the response center or on-site personnel know the answer, but may need reference data to obtain for example, the part #.

Reference data has little value in a self-service environment, where each customer recognizes their issue and is looking for the solution to that issue, which could include what part # will be required.

An organization that is on a journey to increase self-service, must address the conversion of their knowledgebase from a reference knowledgebase to an issue/resolution knowledgebase. This is another example of where change management will be required.

Languages supported

Historically many knowledgebases were in English only. Response center personnel were expected to know their local language which is how they communicated with the customer and then to also know English, which is how they accessed the knowledgebase.

With customer self-service, this does not cut it. For many product types, especially consumer based products, the customer will expect to access the knowledgebase in their local language.

One of the first questions you need to answer is what languages will you need to support. Our company used to require that on-site technicians read English so our service manuals were only in English. Then we started using dealer networks and other service providers in certain countries and quickly found, particularly in Japan, China and Brazil, they did not know English.

Issues/resolutions localized (i.e. translated)

There are multiple approaches companies utilize.

Some companies develop independent knowledgebases per language. This means people in France develop a knowledgebase for issues encountered in France independent of other countries in different languages. This was a fairly standard historical approach which is not very cost effective, nor timely.

Some companies develop their knowledgebase in one language, such as English, and then distribute that knowledgebase to other countries, who decide which articles to translate and arrange for that translation. This also was a fairly standard historical approach, which is also not very cost effective, nor timely.

Some companies develop their primary knowledgebase in one language, such as English, and then use localization companies to either machine translate or perform human assisted translation for either their top issues or all issues. They may machine translate for internal use and then score the machine translation and have human assisted translation for lower scored translations or those being posted externally.

To be effective, a company will have "translation memory" which says that we previously translated this phrase into this, so anytime that phrase is used in any document, it is consistently translated and requires little human assistance.

Knowledge workers

During my career, I was the leader for a group of knowledge workers.

I always found that the product engineers believed they could write the knowledge articles and that was sufficient. But they did not write for grandma and grandpa, they didn't write in a manner that facilitated translation, and adding the proper meta data to improve self-service success was foreign to their thinking.

Within your service environment, you need a knowledge workflow that defines how knowledge is published.

- Who can write it initially (response center or on-site personnel, product engineer)
- Who can post it internally
- Who rewrites it, if necessary based on volume of use, and if it is to be published externally
- Who ensures proper use of trademarks
- Who assigns the meta data
- Who manages the translation process?

- Who manages access rights, i.e. those users allowed access to the knowledge article.

An effective service organization has a role for a knowledge worker.

Remote Service

We have previously described self-service where your customer solves their service issue themselves, either through other parties or through self-service options you have made available.

We also discussed under incident management, that the customer could request service by logging a service incident through your web site or through a widget embedded in your product, or by contacting through telephone or chat your incident handling team.

Let's assume there is now an incident that needs to be addressed by the service provider. For many products, service starts through a remote service capability.

But first, you may be wondering, as a consumer when I call or chat to request service, the person you described as the incident handling team not only logs the service request, but also provides me support. Aren't they providing remote service?

And the answer is yes, the person performing the incident handling function and the person performing remote service can be the same person. But not always.

If your incident workflow is to log the service request and immediately transfer to someone to provide technical support than you might as well have the remote engineer also log the service incident.

Consider a commercial environment, where customers log the service incident through the web, and then they receive a callback by the remote engineer. Or an environment where the service terms indicate that we will have a remote engineer contact you within one hour of logging a service incident even if it is done through a telephone. In these situations, the incident handling function and the remote service function are different people with different skill sets.

Another alternative is an on-site technician calls the customer back and attempts to resolve the issue before going on-site.

Remote service purpose - the purpose of remote service is twofold:

Solve the customer's issue without having to go on-site or sending your product to a depot for service

If it cannot be solved remotely, perform diagnostics that allow you to know what service parts and what skills will be required to fix the issue either by an on-site technician or by sending the product to a depot.

Fundamentals - remember the fundamentals

Self-service can be quicker and is also less expensive than providing remote service.

Remote service will be quicker and less expensive than providing either on-site or depot service.

If on-site service is required, the person that arrives on-site needs the service parts and skills to resolve the issue, or additional trips will be required, which will add cost and increase downtime.

Success rate - as you would expect, software products will have a high success rate with remote service. Remote service success for hardware based products is a function of product design. If the product is designed to allow remote diagnostics and to then allow the customer to replace key wearable parts themselves, remote service can be very successful. If it is difficult to diagnose issues remotely, such as image quality, than remote service is less successful.

Organization - this also means how you organize your remote service capability is a function of your product and how and when the customer requires service. Let's provide a few examples.

- **Response center** – if you have a product with a high success rate with remote service, you will probably do it from a response center. You may even setup multiple response centers globally and tie them together in a follow-the-sun strategy.
- **On-site personnel** – if most of the time you will need to have someone go on-site to service the product, than during normal working hours the on-site person can contact the customer and perform the remote service remotely. You will need to be able to divert after hours calls to a response center. Having the on-site person contact the customer instead of a remote engineer can improve the productivity of the on-site person and also increase customer satisfaction.

Virtual vs. physical response centers

Today's technology allows a response center to be a collection of virtual agents that work in multiple geographies, or even from their home.

The advantage of a virtual response center is it is easier to ramp up and down based on sudden surges in volume (think of the airlines with a major weather delay), and easier to find multi-lingual personnel, since they can reside in different countries.

A virtual response center will not always work. To replicate the customer's issue may require the response engineer to physically be at the company's product, which might only be available at a physical response center.

"Follow-the-sun"

Let's assume we sold our product in only the United States, Canada, and Australia and we needed to provide our customers 24x7 remote service in English.

We could do this from two response centers, one in either the U.S. or Canada and the other in Australia. Australia could cover their daytime hours and the nighttime hours for the U.S. and Canada, with the response center in the U.S. or Canada covering their daytime hours and the nighttime hours for Australia.

Both response centers would only need to be open 12 hours per day, but by a "follow-the-sun" strategy we provide 24 hour coverage.

The two response centers could also support the U.K. with no response center in Europe.

This concept can apply to all countries and all languages, you just have to think through the staffing.

Levels of support – the service industry defines different levels of support, typically L1, L2, L3, and L4. The definitions sometimes differ, but a common definition regarding response centers is:

L1 is the incident handling team function of logging an incident and managing it to ensure service is provided.

L2 is the primary remote engineer who assists the customer remotely

L3 is a response center specialist. When L2 cannot solve the issue, L3 provides assistance based on their greater level of expertise.

When neither L2 nor L3 can resolve the issue it is referred to L4, which is typically product engineering.

A successful remote service strategy measures what percent of incidents can be resolved by L2, what % require L3 and what % engage L4.

A successful company recognizes that if an incident reaches L4, it is a significant customer issue and L4 must "move heaven and earth" to assist in determining a resolution. This means a culture which will divert L4 resources from whatever other tasks they were performing (typically product development) to address the incident.

Staffing – by now, I hope you recognize that staffing a response center, either at a physical location or virtually, is not easy. Factors that need to be included in the staffing model include

- Hours of coverage
- Product skills required
- Product skills available (not everyone will be trained on all products)

- Languages required (don't under estimate this one. For example, we found that Vancouver and Toronto had a broader spectrum of people with multiple languages than U.S. cities, for the types of products we needed to support)
- Distribution of incoming incidents over the hours of coverage
- Distribution of support times, e.g. some issues will take less time than others
- Differences from day to day, e.g. is Monday morning a peak
- Contingencies for sudden spikes in demand, e.g. weather outages

Depot Service

Definition - earlier we defined depot service as your product is sent to a depot where service is performed. There are typically two types of depot service that can be visible to your customers

- **Return for repair** – the customer ships the product to your designated repair facility, where it is repaired or periodic maintenance is performed and then returned to the customer.
- **Advanced unit replacement** – you ship the customer a new or reconditioned unit, and they ship you back (typically in the same box) the non-working unit. The customer does not expect back the non-working unit, which you can repair/recondition and add to a pool for the next customer that needs an advanced unit replacement.

Remember the fundamentals – depot service costs more and takes longer than either self-service or remote service, but will be cheaper than on-site service.

Subassemblies – another use of the depot is when your on-site technician replaces a subassembly at the customer site and sends the subassembly back to the depot for repair/refurbishment at which time it is put back in inventory for the next on-site technician that needs the subassembly. This situation occurs when it will take too long for the on-site technician to diagnose and repair the subassembly at the customer site, or the tools required for diagnostics or repair are only available at a depot.

Strip/salvage – depots can also strip/salvage service parts from equipment no longer used at a customer site. We will talk more about this strategy when we address service parts.

Depot sites – a key question is where are the depots. Let's consider factors important in your decision making:

- **Speed of turnaround**
  - In the U.S., both FedEx and UPS have hub locations that allow shipments picked up today to become available for repair in an overnight window that allows return to the customer tomorrow.
  - Even if service misses the window, there are extra hours available to you to perform the service if your repair depot is in a hub location.
  - Advanced unit replacement strategies have less speed required than when a customer returns a product for repair and expects the repaired product returned quickly.
- **Tool investments**
  - We had on-site technicians that did "bench repair" from our local office, when they did not have an on-site incident.
  - This increased their utilization, but was only possible when there was not significant tool investments for either diagnostics or repair.
- **Government regulations** – Brazil is an example of a country where there is a high importation tax on anything shipped into the country, not to mention delays in getting the parts through customs. A depot inside the country becomes a necessity.

Remote service – most companies that perform depot service on consumer products under warranty require the customer to contact remote service or perform a diagnostic through the web. Why is this?

- **Warranty entitlement** – confirm whether the product is still under warranty. If not, explain to the customer their service options and associated costs.
- **Customer responsibility service** – warranty service does not cover certain conditions caused by the customer, such as a dropped unit that cracks the screen on a device, or a flood that damages the product. Before the product is returned the company will want to tell the customer that these situations are not covered under the warranty
- **No problem found** – too often the depot can find nothing wrong with the unit returned. This just wastes time and cost. Better to do some preliminary diagnostics remotely.
- **Return authorization incident and paperwork** – by sending the customer an email with a return authorization label, there is tracking throughout the process. There cannot be a customer that contends they sent their product back for repair and never saw it again. Plus the depot will know what volume to expect and can staff accordingly.

Outsource options – depending on your product, on a global basis there are generally outsource options to choose from instead of building your own capability internally.

By now I hope you are realizing that customer service is a whole world of its own. There are many books on marketing, sales, product development, manufacturing, finance and accounting and very little on customer service. Providing great customer service is not simple, as I hope you are realizing.

On–site Service

Definition - a service technician is dispatched to the product site to perform service.

Examples – think of all of the times your family has had on-site service.

- We had a pipe freeze in the wall and then burst.
- Our septic system plugged.
- The day before out of town guests were to arrive, the central air conditioning failed.
- As we were leaving the house the car would not start.
- The neighbor smelled gas in their home and evacuated it.
- Our heating system required its annual maintenance call
- This list is endless. We really are a service based society.

What is common across all of these examples – a qualified technician is dispatched to the site requiring service.

Hopefully they were able to bring whatever service parts are required to fix the situation and were able to come in a reasonable time from when the customer requested service.

This did not all happen magically.

The service provider had to have a service plan and execute on that plan.

Volume – from a marketing and sales point of view, we like it when our products rarely fail. From a service delivery standpoint, volume is a friend.

- **Productivity** - volume allows our service technician to be productive. Assume your customer is in a remote geography, such as upper Maine, and worse the customer environment requires 4 hour response time, there are no other customers with your product nearby and service is needed once per week with an average call duration of 4 hours. Will you pay your service technician for 40 hours of work/week and then only require 4 hours?
- **Proficiency** – volume allows the service technician to stay proficient in the product they service. There will be a significant difference in the quality of service provided by the person that has 10 calls/week on your product vs the one with only 1 call/week.
- **Service parts** – if the customer requires 4 hour response to a service situation, you will probably need to have some key service parts locally. Volume allows you to spread this investment over the revenue of multiple units.

Example #1 – during my career, we had a critical expensive product that was used by the financial industry.

To save operations costs they put processing centers in remote locations, such as South Dakota.

The training class for a service technician was 12 weeks, so this was not a candidate for outsourcing. No outsourcer wanted this business.

Worse, most service calls were after hours.

Plus product design did not do a good job of building diagnostics, so the service technician had to swap expensive parts to determine what the cause of the problem was and provide a fix.

The product failed about once per month.

There were other less complex products the service technician serviced to improve their productivity, but for the complex critical product, training cost and part inventory were key factors in whether we would have profitable service. Plus when the local service technician was on vacation, we had to fly in a replacement to be on call.

Welcome to the world of on-site service.

Example #2 – during my career, we had a totally different situation. We were the outsource provider that provided on-site service on behalf of another company. This company sold product to a fast food company that was in most towns in the U.S.

They had their fast food locations contact their internal help desk first whenever they had a service issue.

They monitored how fast we got on site, and whether we fixed the issue in one service call.

They also monitored what service parts were used.

They insisted in their contract negotiations with our partner that all of the top use parts would be stocked so that they could be delivered to any fast food location within 2 hours.

If a part was used, it had to be replaced in inventory so if another situation came up that required it, it was available within 2 hours.

What this really meant was that at the end of the contract, all of this part inventory would need to be scrapped.

Again, welcome to the world of on-site customer service.

Example #3 – during my career, we pursued providing outsource service for a number of different companies.

Servicing electronic billboards was an opportunity we rejected.

One of the requirements was that our service technician would need to have or be able to rent a "cherry picker" that allowed them to provide service at the top of the billboard, wherever it may be, which in the winter may also require us to get a snowplow so our "cherry picker truck" could park next to the electronic billboard.

Why tell you this example? Because the service infrastructure necessary to provide on-site service can be quite expensive. Just think about the electric utility company that services your house. The trucks alone are quite expensive. And in a major storm outage, there is overtime cost, there is the cost of bringing in out of town help from other utilities, etc.

On-site service costs – let's summarize the key costs of providing on-site service

- **Service technician** – labor and benefit costs
- **Management** – costs of managing a geographic diverse workforce
- **Automobile/trucks** – the vehicle themselves, the maintenance on the vehicles, the price of gas, parking fees, highway/bridge fees

- **Tools** – at a minimum a smartphone, plus probably a laptop or tablet, a toolbox, plus any diagnostic tools required
- **Service parts** – local inventory, expedited delivery costs for overnight part shipments
- **Ongoing training** – on new products, on product updates, on better customer relationships, on new systems
- **Burden hourly rate** - typically a company will add up all of the non-service part costs and divide by the number of service hours to get a burden cost per hour of providing service. Remember, they don't get to divide by 40 hours per week, since the typical on-site service technician has downtime when there are no calls, or calls took less time than the schedule expected, etc.

Insource vs. outsource on-site service technicians – this is a key decision companies must make. There are many different factors to consider

Insource

Historically many companies hired their own on-site service technicians and managed them internally.

This ensured they were focused to their products, they were provided proper technical training and just as importantly the company ensured proper customer relation skills.

Historically products were not networked (the internet didn't even exist when the product was designed), so remote diagnostic routines were limited.

In many cases, extensive experience was required to properly diagnose the issue on-site. This was after weeks of training classes (e.g. we had a product that required 6 weeks of classroom training, followed by 6 weeks of traveling with an experienced on-site service technician, followed by another 6 weeks of classroom training)

Many products were mechanical with wearable parts that required predictable service (think of how often the office copier was down waiting for the repair technician).

Ex-military or two year trade school graduates were also excellent sources to hire and train as on-site service technicians.

As indicated above, many companies hired and managed their own on-site service technicians. This may still apply to you if:

- Unique skills are required, especially if extensive training is required
- Volumes are adequate to warrant dedicated workforces
- Outsource options don't want your business or you find their fees are excessive for your type of business (e.g., we serviced product that required proper disposal of chemicals. We found most outsource providers were not interested.)

The changing on-site service business

We all know times change and they have definitely changed regarding on-site service technician options. Let's understand why.

- **Industry standard parts** – instead of unique parts, you probably have a higher % of industry standard parts which can be diagnosed, sourced, and replaced by other than you. A great example of this is Windows based PCs.

- **Electronic parts** – for an individual unit at a customer site, failure is random instead of predictable. One unit in ten may require service in the product's life.
- **Redundancy** – product design woke up to the cost of same day on-site service. By building in redundancy in product design, it allows greater use of next day or scheduled service
- **Software vs. hardware** – More product functions have moved to software from hardware. This is less failure and when failure does occur a higher percent can be addressed remotely
- **Networks** – products are networked. This supports "call home" designs before failure occurs and also allows companies to move work from one machine to another when there is an outage.
- **Remote diagnostics** – if the problem can be diagnosed remotely, and the on-site task becomes replace part a, then the level of training and skill required of the on-site service technician is lowered and different sourcing options are possible.
- **Retirements** – the current workforce of historical on-site service technicians are approaching retirement or retiring. Replacing these people is not easy, given their years of experience, plus new workers are more knowledgeable on software than hardware mechanics.
- **Retiree workforce** – at least in the U.S. it is well known that most retirees did not adequately save for retirement and look for supplemental work options on a part time basis.
- **Stagnant culture** – your processes and culture are so engrained in your organization, but no longer viable, and

people won't change. This could also be true of your cost structure.

- **Service volumes and density** – simply put, historically you had plenty of product density and service volume to support an internal workforce, and this is no longer true

Outsource options – there are 5 outsource options available

- Outsource your existing on-site service technicians
- Supplement your existing on-site service technicians with those from an outsource partner
- Subcontract specific service agreements to an outsource provider
- Subcontract specific tasks, e.g. product installations, to an outsource provider
- Utilize a marketplace to obtain an on-site service technician for a specific service incident

Outsource margin – let's remember that any outsource provider needs to have adequate margin to be a viable business.

Their advantage is that they are a specialist in on-site service and can spread the costs of providing it over greater volume.

They are also interested in volume and density.

Suggesting to an outsource provider that you will service the geographies with high volume and density through your internal resources and want them to service the areas of low volume and density will only proceed if training costs are low and you provide adequate margin to cover their risks. In my experience, neither company is willing to go forward in this scenario

If you outsource your total business, your costs of restarting can be excessive, if your outsource provider fails you. The bottom line is select carefully.

If you establish a contract with an outsource provider, how they are paid becomes important. Let's say you pay them per call, but all parts cost is your responsibility. You just provided the outsource provider an incentive to minimize call duration through excessive replacement of parts. Be careful.

Service marketplaces – this is a very interesting relatively new option to you depending on the skills required to provide service on your product.

Generically, it works as follows:

- The customer contacts your remote services capability to request service.
- You determine what service is required
- You complete a web based work order that indicates where service is required, what skills are required, what service is to be performed, and when, and how much you will pay.
- Your work order is posted to the marketplace. This can be a public marketplace if the skills are generally available, or in advance you could have established a closed marketplace of pre-certified resources.
- One or more qualified resources respond
- You pick the one to do the task.
- The resource completes the task and is paid by the marketplace.
- You pay the marketplace including a surcharge for the use of the marketplace

"WorkMarket" is one company that provides this type of service marketplace.

The advantage of a marketplace such as that described above is the ability to use retirees or college students or others that have the necessary skills on a part time basis and only when you need them.

The service marketplace is going to get a lot more traction going forward. Take advantage of it, where it makes sense.

Service Parts

Definition – effective service requires access to service parts. A common phrase in the service industry is "we need the right part at the right place at the right time". To achieve this for a product that will be serviced globally requires

Part planning & procurement – define sources of supply, enter contracts, negotiate pricing, forecast demand, place orders, address backorders and quality issues, deploy available inventory to global stocking locations

Warehousing – management of stocking locations globally that will allow timely delivery of service parts to service providers within the terms sold to your customers.

Transportation – delivery of service parts to service providers typically in one of three ways

- Expedited same day delivery
- Next day delivery
- Replenishment delivery – 2 or more days

Return logistics – the process of returning parts from the point of service. There are typically three possibilities

- **Return unused parts to inventory** – in anticipation of the service situation, parts 1, 2, and 3 were sent to the customer site, but only part 1 and 2 were required to resolve the service incident. In this case part 3 can be returned to inventory.

- **Return for environmental disposition** – meta data about the service part indicates there is special processing required for its disposal
- **Return for repair/reconditioning** – typically an expensive part, such as a circuit board or an assembly, for which it is too difficult to diagnose or repair at the customer site, but which can be repaired at a depot.

Strip/salvage – every product has a life cycle. At product introduction, service parts are typically new. Later in the product's life, a strip/salvage of used product for service parts is a very viable source of service parts

Material Requirements Planning (MRP) vs. Distributed Requirements Planning (DRP)

If you have studied or worked in manufacturing, your first thought is that the service organization should be using a MRP system to plan their service parts. Unfortunately, you would be wrong.

You would also probably assume that the person that plans parts for manufacturing of finished product is logically the same person that should plan service parts. Again you would be wrong.

Yet, during my career, I constantly ran into this assumption as organizations assumed the company could save money and parts inventory by consolidating the planning functions.

An MRP system typically starts with a forecast, such as everyday next week we plan to manufacture 1000 product xyz, or 5000 for the week. There is then a bill of materials breakdown that says that product xyz has 10 of part 123 and 4 of part 234, and 1 of part 345, etc. This means for the week we will need 50000 of part 123, 20000 of part 234 and 5000 of part 345.

The key point being made here is that the MRP system takes the forecast of finished product, does a bill of materials breakdown and then calculates for each part the # required.

The MRP system will also allow entry of independent demand, e.g. in addition to the 50000 units for part 123 that we will need next week to assemble finished product, we will also need an additional 1000 as independent demand.

That additional 1000 could be for service. But the key question is how anyone forecast that they needed 1000 for service. That is not part of a bill of materials breakdown based on finished product sales.

Forecasting the 1000 for service is the role of DRP, which is a totally different type of toolset than MRP and requires different skills than a person that typically operates in a MRP environment.

Once DRP has forecasted that 1000 of part 123 will be needed next week for service, it can pass that demand requirement to a MRP system for the manufacturing organization that will manufacture the part. That probably will not be the same organization that assembles the finished product. So yes, DRP can and will feed an MRP system, but it will be the MRP system of the parts manufacturer, and not the MRP system for the product assembly organization.

Finally, a service part will have its own bill of materials, namely the part itself and whatever packaging is required for a service part that is not required for a part used in product assembly. (In fact as companies implemented integrated enterprise systems such as SAP, this can actually be a large hurdle. The legacy manufacturing system and the legacy service system both used part #123 to represent the part, but the packaging requirements were different. SAP expects separate part #s).

Part planning

A service organization needs to have a service part planning organization that focuses on what parts are required for service, where are they deployed in our service parts logistics network, what is our forecasted vs. actual consumption, what are our sources of supply for replenishment and how do we work with those sources of supply to obtain the service parts when we need them.

A Distributed Resource Planning (DRP) system provides a total view into our distributed inventory, our forecasts, our suppliers, our lead times, etc. and is a tool required by part planning.

When we introduce a new product to the marketplace, from a service parts perspective there are a number of things that must be done.

Service engineering (their role is discussed in a separate section) must decide which of all the parts in a product will be service parts. Some parts will never fail. Sometimes, service will need to replace a total assembly instead of the individual parts that make up the assembly.

Data about the service part will need to be setup in our service systems, such as part #, description, cost, price, weight, dimensions, etc.

Service engineering will need to provide an initial estimate on part failure rates

Depending on the response time objectives required for our product, expected failure rates, and the cost of the part, part planning and service engineering must then decide where parts need to be stocked.

At product launch we will need all new parts in support of service. For expensive parts, service engineering and part planning need to determine what parts can be repaired instead of purchased new. The repairable parts will have two sources of supply, new parts from the manufacturer and repaired parts from a repair depot. Both will need to be forecasted.

Part planning, in conjunction with procurement, will need to establish sourcing contracts with part suppliers. These will need to address lead times and minimum order quantities, and lot sizes if appropriate.

After product launch, on an ongoing basis, part planning will need to monitor and replan service part requirements based on:

- Updated failure data
- Introduction of product sales into new geographies
- Installed base growth or decline

As the product matures in its lifecycle, there are additional items that will need to be addressed.

Strip/salvage – as the installed base declines, there is an opportunity to strip and salvage parts from units no longer in use. This then becomes a new source of supply.

Alternative suppliers – the original supplier may no longer be in business or now has an excessive price, so new suppliers must be found

Engineering changes

- Changes we make to the product may make some service parts obsolete and require other parts instead. In some cases we may need part #123 for all units manufactured before serial #x and part # 234 for all units manufactured after serial # x.
- The industry may discontinue making parts, requiring us to change our product if we want to continue to provide service.

All time buys – suppliers may decide it is no longer in their interest to make a service part we will continue to need. They tell us it is time for an all-time buy.

As you can see our DRP system needs to allow us to:

- Show visibility of parts in our multi-site logistics network
- Show historical usage and demand (yes both)
- Provide multiple methods to generate the best forecast of our requirements
- Allow us to allocate those requirements between multiple sources of supply, such as new, repaired, and strip/salvage
- Allow us to deploy service parts to our multiple inventory nodes in our global service logistics network

Part stratification – when we think of a product assembly operation, we strive for "just in time" deliveries of the necessary parts. This allows us to eliminate inventory and increase raw material turns.

- **For service parts, we stratify our service parts usage, e.g. "A", "B", and "C" parts.** Companies may have different definitions of "A, B, and C" but for our purposes think of it this way:
  - "A" parts are 5% of our service part #s, but represent 70% of our service part $ usage
  - "B" parts are 10% of our service parts #s, and represent the next 20% of our service part $ usage.
  - "C" parts are 85% of our service part #s, represent 10% of our service part $ usage, but unfortunately also represent most of our service part inventory
- **"A" stratified parts are those few parts which make up most of our $ usage**
  - These are the parts your company will spend the most time on finding ways to reduce unit cost.
  - Typically these are high volume parts and we can work with our suppliers to achieve "just in time" delivery concepts.
  - Instead of "just in time", we really want to think of "just after use", i.e. we used part #123 on a service call today and we need it replaced so it is available for the next service call that requires it.
- **"B" stratified parts are the next echelon of service parts**
  - Many times our repairable parts will be "B" stratified parts.
  - These allow us to focus on inventory value, since repaired parts are less cost than new parts, and we can typically work with our repair depots for "just after use" delivery.
- **"C" stratified parts causes us lots of headaches**

- First, when marketing discontinues sales of a product, manufacturing invariably has excess inventory that they want to dump on service. That is fine for "A" and "B" parts, since in a reasonable period of time, they will be consumed on service calls. But for "C" parts, this is invariably a multi-year supply.
- Second, when we need to buy additional parts, we find that minimum order quantities from our suppliers are a multi-year supply, or worse they want an all-time buy. Plus the cost/unit sky rockets.
- Third, since the last time we purchased a "C" part may have been a few years ago, when we go to purchase more, we may find our supplier no longer makes them. Then we have the cost of finding an alternative supplier.
- Fourth, manufacturing or the supplier may have scrapped necessary tooling or updated the tooling for newer parts that don't allow it to manufacture the service part we require. Now we need to find another supplier, plus tooling.
- All of the above means:
  - Strip and salvage is an alternative that must be pursued. An effective strip and salvage operation includes service engineering talent that determines the proper test procedures to verify part quality and addresses any environmental disposal issues.
  - Service part inventory turns will always be less than what manufacturing can achieve for finished product.

Service part supply dilemma

When a company introduces a new product, they hope that the market reception is "through the roof". Since there are typically constraints on manufacturing, this means every possible part manufactured that is provided to service is one less finished product we as a company can sell.

This puts a tremendous pressure on service to live with less service parts than any reasonable planning model will say is required. The end result is that service does live with less supply and compensates by having high transportation costs.

If the product itself is designed so that most service is next day, then service can consolidate the service parts and ship for next day delivery.

Where life gets difficult is if the service part is required same day, in which case delivery cost can be excessive.

On the other hand if the company assumed high product sales and the product does not meet sales expectations, then invariably excess inventory or committed purchases from our suppliers is dumped to service, and service has a difficult time meeting inventory turn objectives.

Warehousing and Transportation

Any global service organization must address where they will stock service parts.

The answer is really quite simple. You want the minimum number of inventory locations that allow you to meet the service terms you sold your customer. In most cases this is a maximum of two echelons for any country, and if possible one echelon.

Let's understand the key issues in making stock decisions

Response time and uptime commitments – if you sold your customers service agreements that stipulate same day service, then you will need to have some service parts locally.

Let's assume that our objective is that 90% of the time we will get these customers back in operation the same day.

Furthermore we have found that 50% of our service calls do not require service parts.

This means that for the 50% of service calls that do need service parts, we need to have parts locally or that can be delivered the same day for 80% of our parts usage.

Our analysis will probably indicate that is a subset of our "A" and "B" stratified parts, and never our "C" stratified parts.

That is really good news, since we have a high confidence that we will ultimately consume our "A" and "B" parts and having some local stock is little risk on obsolescence.

It also means we stock our "C" parts in a central location that supports next day delivery. The only question is how many of these locations will we need globally. For the U.S. and Canada, one site will work, for most of Europe, one site will work. For the rest of the world we need to do an analysis.

If all of our response time commitments are for next day service, we may not need any parts locally and can put all parts in the same central location as our "C" parts.

Diagnostic capability

If your product is designed so that you can diagnose the issue and determine what parts are required remotely, and if your response time objectives are for next day on-site service, then you can drop ship parts from your central inventory directly to the customer site (or you can arrange to have parts drop shipped from your supplier).

The problem is when your product is not designed to allow diagnostics before the service technician arrives on site. Your customer will not appreciate being told that the service technician arrived on site with no service parts, and will now need to return tomorrow now that the service technician knows what service parts are required.

This is worse if the service technician had to drive a long distance to the customer site or even arrived by plane.

In this case, we are back to the technician having a subset of the "A" and "B" parts when they arrive at the customer site.

This is also an issue if you have outsourced service to a partner who provides the service technician, but expects you to deliver the service parts to the customer site. If you cannot diagnose the incident remotely, you may not be able to outsource the service either, unless your on-site service partner is prepared to stock part inventory.

Central Inventory location

I always found my manufacturing counterparts wanted to co-locate the service part inventory wherever product assembly occurred. Their belief was the company would reduce overall inventory.

From a service perspective, the primary purpose of central inventory is to reliably deliver next day parts to customer sites in support of next day service, and to replenish local inventory that has been consumed on service incidents.

One central inventory globally cannot achieve next day delivery globally, so co-locating is only viable for one region of the world, the region where product assembly happens to be.

But even here there are issues. Let's assume product assembly is in the U.S. on the east coast, and the last pickup by UPS or FedEx is 9 pm for next day delivery. That is only 6 pm on the west coast. That is too early for our west coast customers. We would be better to have our inventory in the hub city of either UPS or FedEx. Last pickup is closer to midnight or even later, a much better delivery window for our west coast customers.

Another issue is that many companies have multiple manufacturing sites, e.g. product xyz may be manufactured on the east coast and product abc on the west coast, all of which must operate until last pickup at a minimum, and potentially be ready to put parts on a next available flight for weekend delivery.

Furthermore, your company will discontinue manufacturing your product long before you can discontinue service. Once product assembly moves onto their next generation product, they lose interest in earlier models.

The bottom line is to determine the best location for where your central service inventory is based on service requirements.

Fill rate

Definition – what percent of the time was the part at the customer site, as required based on the service terms we have with our customer.

For example, if our service terms are for next day service, than what % of the time were the service parts available at the customer site next day?

Fill rate performance - there are a number of factors that impact our fill rate:

- **Correct diagnostics** – if we thought and shipped part 123, but then found we needed part 234, we missed our fill rate
- **Availability** – if central inventory or local inventory did not have the part, then we missed our fill rate
- **Warehouse delay** – even if the part was available to be shipped, we may not have processed it on time or correctly
- **Shipment delay** – even if we delivered it to our carrier on time, there may have been a shipment delay, e.g. caused by weather

Fill rate goal

It is unlikely you will achieve 100% fill rate, primarily because your ability to diagnose 100% in advance is not true, and because you made a decision that you could not afford the inventory investment necessary for 100% availability.

My experience is that central inventory availability needs to be at 99%+ for next day delivery to a customer site (for a down situation) and 95% for replenishment to local stock.

The reason is simple. Your on-site service technicians are the point person with the customer. They get the grief when service parts don't arrive. They need to have confidence in their source of supply or they will take alternative action. They will find ways to stock parts locally, even if it means writing a part off on a service incident for which it was not used, so phantom inventory is available when they need it.

The behavior caused by "lack of confidence" is much larger than you want to believe. We found that we could increase fill rate and lower inventory at the same time, by regaining the service technician's confidence.

My key message is don't allow your logistics team to use too much inventory as an excuse for what is a lousy fill rate with significant downstream costs and loss of customer satisfaction.

Statistical process control (SPC) is a great tool to manage and improve your fill rate performance.

Return Logistics

Definition – the process of returning parts from the point of service. There are typically three possibilities

- **Return unused parts to inventory**
  - o The typical reason is that in anticipation of the service situation, parts 1, 2, and 3 were sent to the customer site, but only part 1 and 2 were required to resolve the service incident. In this case part 3 can be returned to inventory.
  - o A second reason is that part 4 was being stocked locally to meet a same day service commitment that

no longer applies. Part 4 can be returned from local stock to central stock.

- o The key decision is what rules do you establish on what is returned and put back in inventory, what needs to be repackaged, and what is scrapped (either locally or upon return). These rules will be based on part cost, quality, and overall inventory levels.

- **Return for environmental disposition** – meta data about the service part indicates there is special processing required for its disposal
  - o Historically many used parts were disposed of by the customer, or the on-site technician disposed of the parts locally.
  - o Your service engineer needs to evaluate the service parts and determine which ones have components within the service part that have environmental disposition regulations, and have these used parts returned and disposed of per the regulations. The regulations will differ country by country.

- **Return for repair/reconditioning** – typically an expensive part, such as a circuit board or an assembly, for which it is too difficult to diagnose or repair at the customer site, can be repaired at a depot.
  - o My experience is this is a "gold mine" for a service organization. We could typically return, repair, and test certain expensive parts for 30% of the cost of a new part.
  - o Furthermore we setup our repair process so that the economic order quantity was "1".

- o This allowed us to minimize inventory investment, increase inventory turns and most important improve our fill rate.
- o It is very important that engineering define the repair and quality checkout process.
- o Furthermore, when manufacturing discontinues product assembly, instead of scrapping certain tooling, this can be passed to your repair depot.
- **Strip/salvage** – every product has a life cycle. At product introduction, service parts are typically new. Later in the product's life, a strip/salvage of used product for service parts is a very viable source of service parts
  - o My first memory of a strip/salvage operation was an automobile junkyard, that eyesore along our highways.
  - o That was until I visited a different type of automobile strip/salvage operation locally. This site only stored the automobile long enough for it to be dismantled, and the individual parts either put in inventory or recycled.
  - o They had a room of engines, a room of tires, a room of bumpers, etc.
  - o They then had a fleet of trucks which delivered salvaged parts to auto repair locations throughout a fairly large geographic area.
  - o When you strip and salvage any product, there will be some parts you need more than others. The answer is only keep what you will need, and recycle the rest, which is exactly what they did.

- We implemented this same philosophy for a large office product. We learned there was "gold" in a strip/salvage operation, but also challenges.
- First, you must have engineers that determine which parts can be strip and salvaged and what refurbishment/testing process is required before they can be put in inventory. This needs to be rigorous, or you will end up with part quality issues. In some cases, we repainted parts for the visual impact required. Even if they were not repainted, they were cleaned and properly packaged.
- Second, you need recycling experts to help identify the value and proper disposition of the parts you don't need and will be recycled. You will probably be paid more for this recycled material than your total cost of running the strip/salvage operation.
- Third, be careful regarding environmental regulations. The first step in our process was to remove the chemicals that were in the product and put them in a large barrel. There was no issue with shipping the product to our strip/salvage location with the chemicals still in them, but as soon as we put those chemicals from multiple units into a barrel for disposition, we found there were significant EPA regulations regarding the transportation of the barrel.
- The bottom line, is you must be willing to make an investment in a strip/salvage operation, but there is gold there.

Service Engineering

What happened?

My two daughters are engineers, one is a material science engineer and the other is a chemical engineer.

When they were in college, they could have pursued industrial engineering, software engineering, civil engineering or a host of other engineering disciplines.

But whoever heard of a service engineering discipline at any engineering school.

I haven't, yet our need to deliver customer service is critical to product success.

A service engineer is a critical role.

Serviceability

You don't want to have happen to you what happened with one company many years ago. They were bringing to market what they called internally "model B". I naively asked what happened to "model A". I was told they had a product designed and ready to be launched to the marketplace, but the design team had not considered ongoing service and the product was deemed unserviceable. The team had to start all over. While model B and subsequent models were quite successful, they had missed a key window into an emerging market, and were never the "A" player we could have been.

Historically, when products were primarily mechanical, serviceability meant a design that was easy to service once the service technician arrived on site. This meant wearable parts that could be easily accessed, removed and replaced, circuit boards that were on pull out trays to allow easy access and replacement. It meant one standard fastener that allowed one standard tool to open the machine up to allow service.

Serviceability also addresses ease of performing diagnostics. Think about it, what we really want today is a product that when it fails, it tells us why it failed in a way that allows a networked product to "call home", easily understand what is required, and if possible self-correct.

If self-correction is not possible, then access to the knowledgebase by a unique error code will indicate to the remote engineer or the on-site service technician exactly what they need to do.

This just doesn't happen, it takes the discipline of a service engineer.

During product design, the design team needs to agree with what will be an acceptable level of service, i.e. how often service will be required and when service is required, what will be the call duration and parts requirements. As product design occurs, it is the service engineer's responsibility to test and verify that the design parameters will be meet. This intentionally is an adversarial role.

Once the product is launched, it is the job of the service engineer to get the facts on product performance from a service standpoint, and report this to the design team.

Service parts

In the topic on service parts we indicated that it is the service engineer that must decide what parts in the product will be service parts, and then provide the initial estimates on part life.

After launch of the product, the service engineer needs to monitor part usage vs. initial estimates and work with the product design team on any corrective action required.

If the supplier for service parts needs to be changed, it is the service engineer that will need to help evaluate alternative suppliers, and what will be required to ensure adequate part quality.

Knowledge & training

As we discussed under the section on "knowledge management", the service engineer is the subject matter expert (SME) on all knowledge & training created before product launch and also is the person that certifies updates to the knowledge & training after product launch.

Higher level technical support

If the response center engineers or the on-site service technicians cannot resolve the service situation it gets escalated to the service engineer typically before going to product development.

The service engineer may need to fly on-site to provide assistance.

Corrective action

Based on all service incidents, the service engineer identifies what corrective action is required to the product or as input to the next generation of the product to improve service performance.

The service engineer will also identify what corrective action is required of our training programs to improve operational performance?

Also, are their specific response engineers or on-site service technicians that need additional training?

Analytics & Business Management

Typically this will be a small but highly competent team.

For analytics, it is important to have someone (or a few people) that know the service business very well and also know how to manipulate and perform analysis on data.

What's different – a key principle in performing data analysis is asking the question what's different

I previously stated an example, where we found that the differences in reliability between two populations of units installed at customer sites was the geographic susceptibility to thunderstorms.

We determined this by separating the population of well performing units from the non-well performing units and asking over and over, what is different.

What is the same between the two populations may contribute to reliability overall, but does not explain the difference. Concentrate on what is different.

Customer profitability

I highly encourage you to calculate the profitability of each of your customers. Below I will explain a methodology you can use.

Then you need to ask what is different between your profitable customers and your non profitable customers. If done properly, it will be very telling.

In many companies, sales points to service as the reason customers were not profitable. By performing a "what's different" analysis, you may find that

- Service did contribute to customers being unprofitable, but it was not the most significant explanations.
- More significant was discounts that had been given to certain customers
- Or you may find that there were ways the customer's used your product that sales and marketing did not want to address in their pricing models. Examples dealt with customers ensuring their operators were trained, the use of non-qualified consumables, and the type of output generated by the product.

Should all customers be profitable – the answer is absolutely not? Customers purchase service agreements as an insurance policy, i.e. there are very expensive parts that if they fail will cost a fortune, hence the insurance aspect of a service agreement. The good news is you know this too. In your customer profitability analysis, you can identify those expensive parts and determine without them, whether the customer is profitable. With proper "what's different" analysis, you are still able to identify either customers or service plans that need to be addressed.

Calculating customer profitability

Anytime you calculate customer profitability, there are two components, i.e. calculating the revenue and calculating service costs.

Revenue

You want to use earned revenue, as it is reported for taxes.

If you sell a service agreement for $1200/year, then your earned income is $100 per month. If you are reporting profitability for the 2nd quarter then your earned revenue is $300 from the service agreement.

If you provided time & material service, which is invoiced for each service incident, then the earned revenue applies to the quarter in which the service was performed.

If you have professional services, installation services, or educational services, again it is the amount of that revenue that applies to the time period being reported, in our example the 2nd quarter.

As you build your capability to do customer profitability reporting, you want, where ever possible to report your earned revenue at the lowest level possible. For example, if your customer has multiple sites, then you want to report earned revenue, if possible by site. Why, because when you do your "what's different" analysis, you may find that customer site management is "what's different".

For service agreement and time & material revenue, report it at the unit level if possible. This may require that you allocate the overall discount % to each unit. If so, do it.

Service costs

Typically, you have direct service costs and indirect service costs.

Direct service costs are associated with the personnel that provide service to the customer, such as the response center engineer, the depot service repair person, or the on-site service technician.

Direct service costs will also include any service parts consumed as part of providing service.

Indirect costs are all costs that support direct service. This includes the incident handling team, the contract administrators, the part planners and warehouse personnel, the folks that design and maintain your service systems, etc.

Hopefully, you track either hours or minutes of direct time by service incident, as well as all financial service parts consumed to satisfy and complete a service incident. This data should be in your service history file by service incident tied to the customer and unit serviced.

You should keep as individual data fields for each service incident:

- **Labor cost** – direct labor cost of providing service = hours or minutes times the relevant fully burdened cost of direct service
- **Parts cost** – the in-country financial part value of all service parts recorded against the incident.
- **Back office uplift %** - take the costs of all back office costs and ratio them to labor cost. Back office cost includes any administrative support, contract administrators, incident handling team, service systems, management, etc. That is all people related costs of your service organization that do not track time to an incident

or are not in support of service parts. The back office uplift % will be applied to the labor cost of the service incident.

- **Parts uplift %** - Take the costs associated with service parts logistics and ratio them to your parts cost. This will then be a parts uplift % that will be applied to the parts cost of the incident. These costs will include:
- Service parts planning and purchasing costs
- Warehouse space and people related costs
- Transportation costs – expedited and replenishment shipments, as well as any return transportation costs
- Scrap costs – which are not associated with a specific service incident
- Expense parts – if you expense lower value service parts at the time of shipment, and therefore they are not recorded as usage on the service incident, then their cost needs to be part of the part uplift %.
- **Target to actual variance**
- To be beneficial you will want to calculate the cost of an incident at the time service is performed, therefore your fully burdened rate for direct labor and your back office uplift % and parts uplift % will initially be targets based on your operating plan.
- When actual cost is recorded at the end of the month, take your variance % and also apply it to each service incident.

Consumables – in the example service plan in the beginning of this book, we indicated our objective was to measure profitability of service and consumables combined. This means you need to add the cost and revenue of consumables to your model. It's likely this information will be available only at the site and not the unit level. This allows you to calculate profitability with service and consumables combined or service alone.

Using Customer Profitability Data

If you have defined customer profitability data as described above, you have a very important tool for three different audiences and it is even more valuable if the proper "what's different" analysis are performed.

Sales and marketing

- **Global account management** – by aggregating profitability by global accounts with drill down capability to country and site, sales and marketing can better manage the account and address price action or alternative plans, if appropriate.
- **Product marketing** – by aggregating profitability by product and product family, with drill down capability, marketing can also address price action or alternative plans, if appropriate. They can also focus sales on which products have the greater ongoing margin streams.

Service operations

- Can start at the global level and then drill down to country and geography.
- Since service cost data and revenue data are available at the unit level, you can compare profitability by product from one geography to another or from one customer to another, and identify improvement initiatives, such as additional training.

Product engineering

- By aggregating profitability by product and product family, you can analyze where product corrective action is appropriate.

Customer Satisfaction Analytics

- In the section on incident management, we discussed that a good incident management system generates a customer satisfaction survey at the completion of the service incident and then has the response data tied to the incident data.
- I also indicated that a best practice included local management follow-up with dis-satisfied customers.
- We also want to be able to "slice & dice" customer satisfaction data by product, by geography, by global customer and analyze our results including drill down to the specific incident details, especially the comments regarding dissatisfied responses.
- I once had IT tell me that their analytic toolset did not work well with verbiage. In that case, you need a different analytic toolset.
- Some companies that have millions of transactions may argue that they cannot read or process the verbiage customers provide. But, the vast majority of service companies are not in this situation.
- In many customer satisfaction surveys, only a small % of customers ever respond and those that do will be the more negative ones than the positive ones. All the more reason to use analytics to select the population of negative surveys (e.g. product xyz) and read the customer's comments verbatim.

Ranking reports

In the early 1980's I led a service analytics team that was formed to answer top management questions.

Invariably we would get asked to analyze the data about the specific question of the day, and the turnaround time requirements were tight.

Our small team quickly found that we needed some common ranking reports that allowed us to rank our population, then compare the top to the bottom and do a "what's different" analysis. It was a winning strategy over and over. Not only then but now.

Our focus was on "break fix" in an environment where frequent service on a unit was expected.

The three primary ranking reports we needed were

- Unit ranking
- Issue or problem ranking
- Part ranking

Today, I would add to the list

- Customer ranking
- Service provider ranking

Let's talk about each of these.

Customer ranking – two key metrics from my perspective

- Customer satisfaction scores

- Customer profitability
- Customer total cost

Unit ranking

- Customer profitability
- Total service costs
- Total service costs indexed to consumable usage
- Mean time between service incidents

Issue or problem ranking

- # of occurrences
- Total service costs – labor and parts

Part ranking

- Usage
- Total part cost used

Service provider ranking

- Response goal met
- 1st trip complete
- Total service and travel hours

Remember, the goal of a ranking report is to then ask why the top is different than the bottom. It maybe for a very good reason. It may also provide an opportunity to improve performance.

One thing you have to be careful about, especially with a geographic diverse workforce, is stipulating what a metric should be, since your workforce can mysteriously deliver it, when in reality nothing has improved.

Statistical Process Control (SPC)

Using analytics to explain or justify the past with leadership has little value.

Instead you want to use analytics to drive action that improves performance.

Instead too often, I have seen hours spent explaining a 5% drop in a metric this month, only to have it improve 7% next month.

Statistical process control (SPC) allows you to eliminate emotions and focus your team's action to where improvement can be made.

What I used to tell my team is that the SPC process would tell us the mid-point and the upper and lower control limits.

There was no wishful thinking.

If the mid-point was below our objective or the variation of our process was greater than our objective, then we needed to have a get better plan, which we needed to execute.

If our mid-point and variation was consistent with our plan, then as long as the SPC trigger point alarm did not go off, then the team did not need to explain every 5% decline, etc. – that would be a waste of all of our time.

But if an SPC trigger point did go off, then the team needed to move "heaven and earth" to understand whether this was random or really the beginning of a fundamental shift in performance (negative or positive).

When we first started applying SPC principles to service, invariably, the answer I got was that everything was ok, i.e. the SPC trigger was a random event and our process was still "in control". Time after time, this turned out to be incorrect. The SPC trigger was pointing to us "going out of control", and we did not want to admit it. We had to learn to take SPC triggers seriously. And that is when performance really started to improve.

Management

Analytics can tell us how well we are doing and point us to improvement opportunities.

But management (or leadership) has to set the organizational culture to embrace stellar performance.

I have always found that people perform better when they take ownership, particularly ownership for customer satisfaction.

One thing I know that drives me, and most other people I know, crazy is when a person providing service indicates there is nothing they can do, they are just following the policy established by leadership.

This can be particularly bad, when companies outsource part of their service delivery and provide no ability for their outsource partner to deviate, especially when everyone involves knows it makes no sense without a deviation of policy.

The bottom line is that analytics without the proper culture that looks forwards (not backwards) to drive continuous improvement will be a wasted investment in analytics.

This also means that service leadership needs to be at the leadership table. Service has more interaction with the customer than anyone in the company. How does it make sense for a General Manager to have his marketing, product development, finance, sales, and HR leaders at his/her table, and not service leadership?

Contract Administration

Invariably a company has to replace legacy system "A" with a new and improved system "B". Every company I have talked to indicates the biggest challenge is addressing contract administration. We found it to be true ourselves.

Contract administration is how we administer our service contracts, and therefore our service entitlements.

As I indicated before, I was once told that everyone knew what a "full service contract" was, and my response was everyone except the computer. And in today's world, the computer must be able to understand your service terms and what the customer is entitled to receive in the way of service.

Assume your company sells expensive equipment that supports a cyclical business.

- Your customer may want two shift coverage for most of the year, but be 24x7 during the peak season.
- When our processes were manual, it was ok that people understood these differences in what we described as tribal knowledge.
- With customers now interacting with our computer systems, our service system must understand this difference.
- This means your contract administration team will have more work, not less going forward. In the past they could have entered a contract to the system and in a text field indicate that the customer had 10 months of 2 shift coverage and 2 months of 24x7 coverage. Humans would have understood this. The computer does not. Now they will

need to have an effective and end date for the 2 shift coverage and a separate effective and end date for the 24x7 shift coverage.

- This also means you want to sell this all upfront. It will be more work on your contract administrators, if you initially sold 2 shift coverage for 12 months and then come back and want to change two months to 24x7 coverage. With toolsets like SAP that would mean cancel the initial 12 month contract and now enter two new separate contracts, one of 10 months with 2 shift coverage, and one of 2 months with 24x7 coverage.
- We will talk later about change management. Getting sales to change their thinking will be part of having a cost effective contract administration team.

I cannot stress enough that with the integrated systems of today vs. either the manual or separate systems of the past, times have changed.

In the past, you probably had or even still have a contract administration system separate from your service delivery system.

This means they did not have to agree. In fact there were times when sales did not want them to agree. If this was a very valuable customer, maybe sales wanted to sell them a 2 shift contract and tell the customer we would provide 24x7 coverage.

- The contract administration system indicated 2 shift coverage
- The service delivery system indicated 24x7 coverage
- And everyone was happy.

- That was until the contract administration capability and the service delivery system were integrated into one system. Now they had to agree.
- This means the integrated system has to indicate that the customer is entitled to 24x7 coverage, but receives a discounted price to the equivalent price of 2 shift coverage. This also means that discount is now visible to management, something the sales rep may not be happy about.

Worse still if you have complex equipment with many component options, your installed base may be relatively small, but each installation is relatively unique, and to get the sale, each customer deal is different. You may even be doing all of your pricing on a spreadsheet. However you are doing this, your contract administrators need to enter into your service delivery system the key data that allows service delivery and the computer to know service entitlement.

What all of this means is you want your contract administrators working closely with sales very early in the sales process, so the deal can be structured in a way that facilitates ongoing contract administration. Remember it is not only the initial sale, but service will have ongoing service agreement renewals to process.

In the sample service plan, I indicated that preferred pricing was a cost per widget for which the cost included the cost of the consumables and service combined.

- There are other scenarios. When office copiers were introduced, the pricing plans included the copier, the consumables and service, all combined.

- When you present your customer bundled pricing, internally you need to be able to do a bill of materials breakdown, i.e. for every $1 of revenue, what % is attributed to service, what % is attributed to consumables, etc.
- There are multiple reasons you need to do this
  - In some countries, such as the U.S., if service revenue is greater than x% of revenue, it must be reported separately.
  - If you want the benefit of customer profitability reporting with the ability to distinguish whether the improvement opportunity is equipment, consumables, or service, you need to be able to determine the profitability of each.

Your contract administrators must also process renewals, and typically also process your monthly, quarterly, or annual invoices.

Service agreement renewals are very important to your business, since they represent ongoing revenue over many years. This means, when you first sell the customer the product itself and the initial service agreement, in a competitive bid type situation, where a discount is necessary for the sale, you want to discount the product itself and not service, since the product will be a one-time sale and the service agreement will renew year after year.

There are fundamentally two types of service agreements:

- **Traditional service agreements** - have a defined effective date and a defined expiration date. If the customer does not renew the service agreement before the expiration date, then any service after the expiration date is on a time & material basis.

- **Evergreen service agreements** – have a defined effective date, but no expiration date. Instead the terms indicate that the service agreement will remain effective until the customer provides x days (typically 60 days) advance notice that they wish to terminate the service agreement. Part of the terms and conditions of the evergreen service agreement will specify when and by how much the price can change over time.

Evergreen service agreements are effective if invoicing occurs on a monthly or quarterly basis, since the customer just keeps receiving invoices like they did last month or last quarter. When an evergreen contract is invoiced annually, it is easy to perceive it as a traditional service agreement.

Evergreen contracts can still require work on an annual basis by the contract administrators.

Many customers will require a purchase order # (PO#) with an invoice, and many will expire on an annual basis. The contract administrator will need to contact the customer for a new PO.

Systems such as SAP have no concept of an evergreen contract. When you setup the customer's contract, you must enter an effective date and expiration date. Therefore the contract administrator will need to enter a new contract to the system, even though the customer is told they must give 60 days' notice to cancel the service agreement.

Change Management

Throughout my career, I would encounter the latest "buzz word" developed by consultants to allow them to extract from us a lot of consulting $s. The phrase "change management" fit this scenario very well. Historically we had done it very well. We were not smart enough to call it "change management".

Let me give an example. Like many service companies in the 1980's we operated in the U.S. with a local incident handling team that supported an operation of 80-120 on-site service technicians. The customer called the incident handling team, they logged the service incident, and they communicated with the on-site service technicians their service incidents.

In reality the incident management team ran the operation. They told the on-site service technician which incidents to take and in what order.

There were a number of issues leadership had with this approach:

- We had successful products in the marketplace and we were rapidly growing. Each local operation had their own minicomputer and we were constantly needing to reorganize the workforce, causing a lot of work moving data from one minicomputer to another.
- Each local incident handling team operated 8-5 local time. We were introducing products that required 24x7 coverage and this model did not support it.

- We were highly dependent on the "tribal knowledge" of the members of the incident handling team. This naturally put us at risk, but even more so in a timeframe of rapid growth.
- Our newer products allowed remote support, which would operate on a U.S. wide basis, and not on a local basis.

Leadership decided to consolidate the local incident handling teams into two redundant national teams with the implementation of a new central service support system.

Leadership made three fundamental decisions:

- The new central incident handling team would be a communicator to the on-site service technician, and not the decision maker.
- The on-site service technician was asked to run their territory as if it were their own business, and if they needed help (to meet the on-site response time goals), they needed to ask. They were also asked to develop a close working relationship with the customer just like they would if it were their own business.
- The new service support system had to have the information within it that would allow the incident to be assigned to the proper on-site service technician (previously tribal knowledge) and have escalation processes to ensure all customers were serviced appropriately.

When consultants talk about the importance of "change management", this was a very large example. You better manage the change process correctly, or it will fail. Think about all of the folks that would want to see this fail (and help make it fail).

- **Local incident handling teams** – many of which would lose their job
- **On-site service technicians** – some would be very happy with their greater role of managing their territory, but others were comfortable with how it had been
- **Local supervision** – a central incident handling team meant common processes instead of the previous flexibility where each local manager could make decisions unique to their operation
- **Local sales** – they too, knew personally the local incident handling team, and were used to giving instructions to them about how to handle specific customers.

This is also an example of where change management was handled very well.

Key service personnel (on-site service technician, incident handling team, and supervision) were assigned to the process and system design team to ensure an appropriate design.

Throughout the process, there were ongoing communications to keep people informed.

Human resources was actively engaged from day 1, given the impact on job responsibilities and staffing.

Contingency plans were developed to address multiple scenarios, e.g. what happens if local incident handling team members started to resign in high numbers.

Service leadership actively reviewed key elements of the design, and then were the first to go through training.

Local supervision traveled to the new central incident handling team before their live data to see the operation in person and develop personal relationships with the new central team.

When the local operation converted to the new system and to being handled by the new central incident handling team, the second level manager responsible for the 80-120 on-site technicians of his/her geography, spent the week before conversion and the week after conversion at the new central incident handling team. This allowed any issues to be worked jointly, and also for them to be able to tell their team, that yes these people do know what they are doing and it does work.

We had so many local operations to convert, it took a year and a half to accomplish. We started with the first location, and then waited 8 weeks to do a second, and then waited another 4 weeks to do the third. This allowed us to stabilize the new system and operation. We then started doing a local operation every weekend (that was not a significant holiday weekend), and then moved to two operations every weekend.

The example above was from the late 1980's, and as I said before, change management was critical to our success.

Go forward 30 years. By now, many companies have consolidated their service operations within a country or even within a region of the world.

Now we need to be talking about globalization and process integration. That means we have an integrated system that addresses all service functionality and it operates on a global basis.

Stop and think about the change management challenges.

There are many different theories on how to design and develop new service processes and systems.

A common one is to pick a location and/or product, and design and implement the new capability for them, and then adjust it as you go to new geographies or new product programs. From a globalization standpoint, this approach will fail.

I led a team to implement new service processes and systems on a global basis.

One of our core software components was SAP. We met with SAP and they told us we could design the system for one country, but we would die from administration by the time we were done. As an example, we were told we needed to define our service agreement constructs on a global basis first, and then ask what needed to be different locally. We could address the local component when we implemented that local country, but the global component needed to be as "sold as a rock" and in place with the first country implemented.

We had to engage a global team upfront, which we did. This meant global trips, it also meant the teams had to have multiple conference calls to get input from all time zones. It is not easy, especially when you are telling some geographies it is important to be engaged now, but you probably won't be implemented for a few years.

As I said earlier it took 6 months for a global team to agree that 95%+ of our service agreements were really very similar and could be defined in a consistent manner globally. For successful change management, this people investment is necessary.

In our company, the U.S. was the largest country and therefore tended to be the first to be implemented to a new system.

With our globalization endeavor, we decided to implement elsewhere first. This was a significant project that was being managed from the U.S. and we decided to implement in the U.K. first and Australia second. Our rationale was all around change management

- o Historically we had implemented in the U.S. first, and therefore the solution implemented never had buy-in globally.
- o Our European manager was very engaged and wanted to be first.
- o We wanted to implement a country in a second region as quick as possible. The design team leadership was U.S. based so we knew we would have U.S. engagement. By implementing first in the U.K. and second in Australia, we would have continued engagement of those regions and continued ownership of the design.
- o This was a significant system initiative. The U.K. and Australia were both English speaking, so language would not be an issue during system stabilization.
- o Europe had worker council and data privacy issues which were more stringent than in other regions. We wanted to make sure our design addressed these.
- o The U.K. had some overlap of time zones with the U.S. and was easier to fly to than Australia, especially during initial system stabilization.

For success, whenever you change your system processes, a key to success will be to think through what will be required to manage change.

Service Systems

I spent my career in service. One thing I learned early was if you really want to know how a service organization operates, look at their service systems.

Service systems embody the processes that the organization uses to provide customer service.

Service processes and systems really go together. They cannot be separated. This is particularly true today when our customers and partners expect to interact with us through the web or an app. We lose the ability of a human being that shields us from what maybe dysfunctional systems and processes by which we really operate.

A key question any service organization faces is how we justify ongoing investment and modernization of our service processes and systems.

Any company will not survive in the marketplace if they do not use R&D to develop or acquire new products. For service, R&D is the continual renewal and improvement of our service processes and systems. It is really that simple.

If as a service organization, we want to be viable as a provider of third party service to other companies, if those companies are global, we had better invest in making our service processes and systems global.

In many third party service situations, the third party sells the service agreement, and takes and logs the service incident. They may even provide the remote service, and want us to be their feet on-site. If this is the case, our systems better be able to interact with their systems. Our systems must also be able to accept a work order from them, create a service incident in our system, and keep them appraised of our service response.

The bottom line is our service systems cannot be limited to supporting ourselves, but instead must be designed to easily interconnect with our customer's and partner's systems. I question how many of us can really say we do that well.

When I first started out in service many years ago, I became a lead on a project to implement the first mini-computer based service system that did not require an operator for overnight processing to occur. The mini-computer supplier was astounded at what we had accomplished.

Back then, you sat down with leadership and determined what they wanted to accomplish, and designed your system accordingly.

While this resulted in a unique system, it embodied the service processes the leadership wanted.

Move forward to today, and the first question and assumption is we will implement a package developed for the industry. The software provider will be quick to indicate their system embodies industry best practices. What this really means is their system reflects what they designed and are now touting as best practices. Whether they are best practices is open for debate.

More importantly, instead of asking service leadership how they want to operate, now the team is to learn what the out of box system supports and then tell service leadership this is how they are to operate.

This is really tough, and is a key reason why leadership will need to endorse change management if the new or improved system is to be successful.

I have had people say to me we utilize SAP software, or we utilize Oracle software or the other options that are available. Then the words get dangerous, i.e. for tight integration, the service systems should be on the same platform to ease system integration across company functions.

The reality is a service organization can no longer be successful if it doesn't integrate with its customer's, partner's and supplier's systems. We cannot dictate what systems they use, so we better be able to integrate well to other company's software.

Earlier I gave the example of a third party service relationship, where the third party logged the service incident and performed remote support to their customers, but if on-site service was required, they wanted to send us a work order specifying where we needed to provide service. This is where some of the fully integrated systems have an issue. They expect that the customer is in your customer master, the product is defined in your product master, etc., when in reality this work order is the only time we ever go to that customer's site. The bottom line, don't be fooled into thinking that one software package will be better for your company since it will ease integration. It may actually make integration with your customers, partners, and suppliers more difficult.

When we started our system globalization issue, we had a number of consultants that wanted us to engage them, and in hindsight provided wrong advice.

First, they wanted us to document and flowchart all of our current processes. We had 4 regions of the world and multiple product families, each with independent processes and systems. Our customers were telling us they wanted to operate with one company, not one for each region/product family combination. We would have spent a lot of $s with these consultants, when the message we really had to send, and did send, was work together and help us design the go forward process to which we will all operate.

Second, they told us, since we were integrating processes and systems, that it would be better to redo all system components at once, i.e. replace over 90% of your service systems for a country on one day. We actually tried this with our first country implemented and found it was too much for the organization to embrace at one time.

The intent was to reduce the IT investment in temporary bridges between a new and old system. This was unrealistic. As an example, think about any highway improvement. There is always an investment in temporary structures for divided highways, traffic crossovers, etc. Why would the IT world be so different?

As I mentioned earlier, contract administration is the area of most difficulty, but not the area with the largest payback. We learned we had to go live integrated to our old contract administration system, even though that was not easy.

I have been engaged in or led major service system initiatives throughout my career. I found there are some key items required for success:

Project leadership – must have a vision of the future and one they can articulate to the team. The vision must be a significant step forward, the status quo is not sufficient. They must be respected by the team and the organization impacted by the changes to be implemented.

Simple words – charters, vision statements, etc. with lots of words are useless. There are 5-6 key words or phrases for which the team will remember and can always test against. Think of

- **24x7** – today we would expect this, but in the 1980's if you told a team the system had to operate 24x7, it was a major challenge, and those simple words were used to test every element of our design.
- **Customer centric** – as an organization we needed to change from being internally centric by region or product family to be customer centric in all of our process design.
- **Web enabled** – some of our legacy systems had been in place before the web. How they were designed and how we needed to design now were totally different.
- **Partner integrated** – we recognized that not all components of service delivery would be fulfilled by us, so we better be able to integrate our processes to our partner's processes for a seamless customer experience.
- **Global** – we had global customers and they expected us to operate in a common manner across countries.

The team – made up of the best people in the organization even though it may be over a year before the first implementation. If it doesn't hurt to assign the person to the team, it is probably not the right person.

Team makeup – a combination of service and IT people, each with defined areas of responsibility.

"Shoot for the moon" – the team needs to strive to deliver something significantly better than today. A compromised design is a sub-optimal design and will result in the status quo.

"No excuses" – too often I found that there was sign-off on specifications, and when delivered, it did not work, at which point there was finger pointing back to we delivered to the signed off specifications. On my most successful project, I did not allow sign-off as an excuse. You were expected to learn the service business so well, so if there was a problem (and there always will be), you took immediate ownership and corrected it, and better yet, had thought of the issue and resolved it in your original design.

"Good design is free" – just like "quality is free", so think it out now before we invest, instead of needing to do a retrofit later.

When it is time to implement the new or improved system, ideally you will implement it to one country or one product family first so you can stabilize it with a smaller team. It is important that the team to be implemented second participate in the implementation of the first team, likewise the third team should participate with the second implementation, etc.

Test for Understanding

No book titled "Service 101" would be complete if we didn't have a section for you to test whether you understand what you have read. For each statement below, indicate whether it is true or false.

The next section of the book will provide the answers.

True or false:

1. A service plan is explained in a document that summarizes all key aspects of your products and how you will support them.
2. Customer expectations and how you want to be positioned in the marketplace drive your service strategy, which then drives your service plan.
3. A company's service system embodies the service processes the company utilizes in servicing their customers.
4. Service can be included in a bundled price to the customer, and never needs to be reported separately in the company's financial reporting.
5. It is more important to get the price we need for our product, even if we discount service to get the order.
6. It is important to give the same response time options to our time & material customers that we provide our service agreement customers.
7. Having effective remote support will lower the inventory investment in service parts.
8. The web has enabled service organizations to improve their productivity.

9. The cost of providing service is heavily influenced by product design.
10. All service organizations should operate as profit/loss organizations.
11. The customer is the person that buys our product.
12. A critical component of incident management is ensuring the service incident is addressed appropriately.
13. Knowledge access rights define whether person x is entitled to access knowledge y.
14. There are three types of remote service, namely "self-updating", "dial home", and "call out".
15. Depot service only allows customers to return product for repair.
16. The service parts function addresses part planning & procurement, warehousing, and outbound transportation.
17. One function of a service engineer is to be the subject matter expert that defines how the product is to be diagnosed, and what the repair procedure will be.
18. The term serviceability means ensuring during product design that the product can be effectively serviced.
19. All parts in a product must be stocked as a service part.
20. If a service agreement is sold for $1200/year, and is effective on July 1st, then $1200 can be reported as earned income in July.
21. A customer on an evergreen service agreement will keep the same service cost/year until the agreement is terminated, typically by giving the customer 60 days advance notice.
22. Customers rarely decide on what product to buy based on service.
23. As a company we should support the next generation product the same way we supported the previous generation.

24. Everything starts with the customer. For a good service plan, you need to understand their objectives, their business model, and their environment in detail.
25. The customer's use of third party consumables in our product cannot impact the price we charge for service.
26. We can tell our on-site service technician to account for seasonality in their service response to a customer on a service agreement.
27. If we sell a service agreement with a 4 hour on-site response goal, then penalties are invoked if the on-site service technician is not on-site within 4 hours.
28. When a customer purchases a service agreement, all service is included at no charge to the customer.
29. Customers expect us to train them on product use as part of the fee they paid to purchase our product.
30. On-site warranty service is typically provided during standard business hours.
31. A customer must purchase time & material service from the customer that sold them the product.
32. All self service is provided through the product manufacturer or their partner.
33. As more customers request service through the web, the role of the incident handling team has changed to handling exceptions, and providing oversight that all incidents are serviced appropriately.
34. Global companies can be more productive if they operate their incident handling team in a "follow the sun" configuration.
35. The two factors that determine what staffing is required for your incident handling team is call duration and the statistical distribution of incoming calls.

36. When designing a new service system, incident handling and the knowledgebase are independent of each other, especially with all of the knowledge available through the web.
37. When an incident is completed and closed, the customer should always receive an invitation to complete a web based customer satisfaction survey.
38. A knowledgebase that is primarily reference data indicates the company has not embraced best in class knowledge principles.
39. All knowledge articles should be certified before being published on a company's web site.
40. A software company can eliminate their need to provide customer support by allowing the community to provide it instead.
41. How knowledge is written and understood by people that use it every day can be different than a customer that accesses it just once.
42. Meta data is data about something.
43. Localization is a process by which knowledge is translated into multiple languages.
44. A knowledge workflow defines how (steps required and by whom) knowledge is published.
45. The remote service engineer is also the person that logs the incident and performs the functions of the incident handling team.
46. Remote service will be quicker and less expensive than providing depot or on-site service.
47. The purpose of remote service is to fix the customer's issue remotely.

48. In some cases, remote service can be performed by a virtual team that includes on-site service technicians that are not currently dispatched to on-site service incidents.
49. A successful company recognizes that if an incident reaches L4, it is a significant customer issue and L4 must move "heaven and earth" to assist in determining a resolution.
50. Governmental regulations can impact whether a company needs to perform depot service within a country.
51. If a customer drops the product during the warranty period, it will be fixed at no charge.
52. From a service delivery standpoint, volume is a friend since it allows greater productivity of the service technician, allows the service technician to maintain service proficiency, and supports investment in service parts.
53. Service marketplaces now exist that allow companies to source on-site service technicians on demand.
54. Return logistics are required to return unused parts to inventory, to return used parts for environmental disposition, and to return parts for repair/remanufacturing.
55. A material requirements planning system is adequate for planning service parts.
56. Later in a product's life cycle, a strip/salvage of used product is a very viable source of service parts.
57. Forecasting service parts is typically accomplished as independent demand, while parts for product assembly is typically a bill of materials breakdown of forecasted product sales.
58. The skills required to successfully plan and procure service parts are identical to the skills required to plan and procure parts for finished product assembly.

59. Depending on the response time objectives for our product, expected failure rates, and the cost of service parts, decisions will need to be made on where service parts are stocked.
60. For service parts, a few parts will make up most of our usage, but the parts with low usage will make up most of our service parts inventory.
61. When deciding where to stock service parts, you want the minimum number of stocking locations that allow you to meet the service terms you sold your customers.
62. It is best to co-locate service part inventory at the same site where product assembly occurs.
63. Service part fill rate performance is impacted by product diagnostic capability, part availability, warehouse delay and shipment delay.
64. Companies need to strive for 100% fill rate of service parts.
65. We can always ask the customer to dispose of used service parts.
66. In setting up a strip/salvage operation, you must consider how you will dispose of chemicals.
67. During product design, the design team needs to agree on what will be an acceptable level of service.
68. The service engineer, as the subject matter expert, is the best person to write knowledge articles.
69. A key principle in performing data analytics is asking the question "what's different".
70. Service needs to be profitable for each and every customer serviced.
71. Effective customer profitability analytics allows drill down by customer, by geography, and by product.

72. Sales and marketing, service operations, and product engineering will each find value in analyzing customer profitability.
73. Ranking reports are effective tools to allow us to separate high performing and low performing populations to better understand causes of customer service.
74. Service organizations can embrace statistical process control.
75. Contract administration is how we administer our service contracts, and therefore our service entitlements.
76. Traditional service agreements have a defined effective and expiration dates. Evergreen service agreements have a defined effective date, but remain in place until the customer provides advance notice to cancel.
77. Proper "change management", especially by leadership, will determine whether an improvement project is successful.
78. Globalizing service processes has minimum requirements for change management.
79. For service, R&D is the continual renewal and improvement in our service processes and systems.
80. Service systems must be designed to easily interconnect with our customer's, partner's and supplier's systems.

Test for Understanding – Answer Key

1. A service plan is explained in a document that summarizes all key aspects of your products and how you will support them. *(True)*
2. Customer expectations and how you want to be positioned in the marketplace drive your service strategy, which then drives your service plan. *(True)*
3. A company's service system embodies the service processes the company utilizes in servicing their customers. *(False, this should be true, but service companies will allow manual workarounds to overcome system deficiencies)*
4. Service can be included in a bundled price to the customer, and never needs to be reported separately in the company's financial reporting. *(False, some countries require service revenue to be reported separately if it represents more than x% of revenue)*
5. It is more important to get the price we need for our product, even if we discount service to get the order. *(False, service is an ongoing revenue stream while the product sale is typically a one-time sale. Discount the one-time revenue to maintain a higher ongoing revenue stream.)*
6. It is important to give the same response time options to our time & material customers that we provide our service agreement customers. *(False, why would a company incur the cost of providing expedited options to a customer that has not committed to utilizing those services through a contractual arrangement)*

7. Having effective remote support will lower the inventory investment in service parts. *(True)*

8. The web has enabled service organizations to improve their productivity. *(True)*

9. The cost of providing service is heavily influenced by product design. *(True)*

10. All service organizations should operate as profit/loss organizations. *(False, every organization must make this decision, but most companies do establish service as a profit and loss entity)*

11. The customer is the person that buys our product. *(False, as defined in this book the customer is the person that uses our product, which can be different than the person that purchased it).*

12. A critical component of incident management is ensuring the service incident is addressed appropriately. *(True)*

13. Knowledge access rights define whether person x is entitled to access knowledge y. *(True)*

14. There are three types of remote service, namely "self-updating", "dial home", and "call out". *(False, e.g. there is also telephone and chat support)*

15. Depot service only allows customers to return product for repair. *(False, many companies have advanced unit replacement as a second option).*

16. The service parts function addresses part planning & procurement, warehousing, and outbound transportation. *(True, but remember it also includes return logistics and strip/salvage)*

17. One function of a service engineer is to be the subject matter expert that defines how the product is to be diagnosed, and what the repair procedure will be. *(True)*

18. The term serviceability means ensuring during product design that the product can be effectively serviced. *(True)*
19. All parts in a product must be stocked as a service part. *(False, some parts never need replacement in a service situation, and others are replaced only as a higher level assembly)*
20. If a service agreement is sold for $1200/year, and is effective on July 1st, then $1200 can be reported as earned income in July. *(False. In this example, earned revenue would be $100 per month, with $100 reported in July and a total of $600 reported in the current calendar year)*
21. A customer on an evergreen service agreement will keep the same service cost/year until the agreement is terminated, typically by giving the company 60 days advance notice. *(False, every agreement has a set of terms and conditions. The terms can specify that the service provider is allowed to increase the price over time)*
22. Customers rarely decide on what product to buy based on service. *(False, it depends on the type of product and the importance the customer places on after sales support)*
23. As a company we should support the next generation product the same way we supported the previous generation. *(False, technology advancements allow new and better support models. If our next generation product supports web based diagnostics and our previous generation did not, we miss an opportunity for providing better service if we stick with the past)*
24. Everything starts with the customer. For a good service plan, you need to understand their objectives, their business model, and their environment in detail. *(True)*

25. The customer's use of third party consumables in our product cannot impact the price we charge for service. *(False, but we better be able to demonstrate the impact the third party consumables have on service cost, and that it is different with our consumables. A key question will be whether both sets of consumables are within the specifications we specified for our product. If so what justification do we have to charge more?)*

26. We can tell our on-site service technician to account for seasonality in their service response to a customer on a service agreement. *(False, this was true in the past, but in today's world the customer can interact with us through the web, and if the service incident was logged at 2 am, we may not tell the on-site service technician until 8 am if our service system did not also account for the different coverage during the seasonal timeframe)*

27. If we sell a service agreement with a 4 hour on-site response goal, then penalties are invoked if the on-site service technician is not on-site within 4 hours. *(False, our service agreement terms will specify that it is our objective and intent to attempt to respond within 4 hours. Rarely will we see penalties built into the contract)*

28. When a customer purchases a service agreement, all service is included and no charge to the customer. *(False, it all depends on the terms of the service agreement. Companies typically exclude what we call customer responsibility service, such as dropping the equipment, operating it out of specifications, damage caused by flooding, etc. Customers can also purchase labor only service agreements and pay for the parts as they are needed. Each service agreement will*

have a set of terms and conditions that determine whether any particular service is billable or not)

29. Customers expect us to train them on product use as part of the fee they paid to purchase our product. *(False, once again it depends on the terms of sale. A company can include training as part of the price of the product purchased, or it can sell educational services as a separate product)*

30. On-site warranty service is typically provided during standard business hours. *(True, typically customers that require after hours service can buy an extended warranty)*

31. A customer must purchase time & material service from the customer that sold them the product. *(False, customers have the choice of who to purchase service from, especially time & material service. Think of all of the automobile service that is not done through the dealer)*

32. All self service is provided through the product manufacturer or their partner. *(False, communities will provide support to their members. Also many people will ask a relative or friend first before contacting the manufacturer)*

33. As more customers request service through the web, the role of the incident handling team has changed to handling exceptions, and providing oversight that all incidents are serviced appropriately. *(True)*

34. Global companies can be more productive if they operate their incident handling team in a "follow the sun" configuration. *(True)*

35. The two factors that determine what staffing is required for your incident handling team are call duration and the statistical distribution of incoming calls. *(False, these are two factors that are required to determine staffing, but*

others are also required. Specifically, what customer hold time is acceptable, and what skills are required of the incident handling team)

36. When designing a new service system, incident handling and the knowledgebase are independent of each other, especially with all of the knowledge available through the web. *(False, first, best practice today indicates they should be fully integrated. Second, not all knowledge is available to customers through the web, only the knowledge we grant them access rights. There will always be knowledge that a service organization does not want public, which will be entitled and available to the response center engineers and the on-site service technicians)*

37. When an incident is completed and closed, the customer should always receive an invitation to complete a web based customer satisfaction survey. *(False, in many consumer situations the answer will be true, but in commercial situations with frequent service requirements, sometimes even daily, a company needs to define rules on how often the same person can receive a survey)*

38. A knowledgebase that is primarily reference data indicates the company has not embraced best in class knowledge principles. *(True)*

39. All knowledge articles should be certified before being published on a company's web site. *(False, each company must make the trade-off of the time required for certification and the risks associated with non-certified knowledge. If non certified knowledge is published to the web, it should be noted as "non certified")*

40. A software company can eliminate their need to provide customer support by allowing the user community to provide

it instead. *(False, a community offloads part of the support costs, but not all)*

41. How knowledge is written and understood by people that use it every day can be different than a customer that accesses it just once. *(True)*
42. Meta data is data about something. *(True)*
43. Localization is a process by which knowledge is translated into multiple languages. *(True)*
44. A knowledge workflow defines how (steps required and by whom) knowledge is published. *(True)*
45. The remote service engineer is also the person that logs the incident and performs the functions of the incident handling team. *(False, in some cases the remote service engineer does also log the service incident, but where companies log the service incident and then have a remote service engineer contact the customer, e.g. within an hour, they are not the same person. Also there are additional functions, such as incident oversight, not performed by the remote service engineer)*
46. Remote service will be quicker and less expensive than providing depot or on-site service. *(True)*
47. The purpose of remote service is to fix the customer's issue remotely. *(False, we would all love it if remote service always fixed the customer issue. There are situations where remote service diagnoses the issue so service parts can be shipped to allow the customer or an on-site service technician to fix the issue)*
48. In some cases, remote service can be performed by a virtual team that includes on-site service technicians that are not currently dispatched to on-site service incidents. *(True)*

49. A successful company recognizes that if an incident reaches L4, it is a significant customer issue and L4 must move "heaven and earth" to assist in determining a resolution. *(True)*

50. Governmental regulations can impact whether a company needs to perform depot service within a country. *(True)*

51. If a customer drops the product during the warranty period, it will be fixed at no charge. *(False, most warranty terms indicate that if the customer damages the product, then the customer must pay for the service to fix it)*

52. From a service delivery standpoint, volume is a friend since it allows greater productivity of the service technician, allows the service technician to maintain service proficiency, and supports investment in service parts. *(True)*

53. Service marketplaces now exist that allow companies to source on-site service technicians on demand. *(True)*

54. Return logistics are required to return unused parts to inventory, to return used parts for environmental disposition, and to return parts for repair/remanufacturing. *(True)*

55. A material requirements planning system is adequate for planning service parts. *(False, there are lots of reasons, including return of parts for repair/remanufacturing and using strip/salvage as a source of supply)*

56. Later in a product's life cycle, a strip/salvage of used product is a very viable source of service parts. *(True)*

57. Forecasting service parts is typically accomplished as independent demand, while parts for product assembly is typically a bill of materials breakdown of forecasted product sales. *(True)*

58. The skills required to successfully plan and procure service parts are identical to the skills required to plan and procure

parts for finished product assembly. *(False, a service parts planner must address the geographic placement of service parts, plans independent demand, and must plan for part repair/remanufacturing and strip/salvage)*

59. Depending on the response time objectives for our product, expected failure rates, and the cost of service parts, decisions will need to be made on where service parts are stocked. *(True)*

60. For service parts, a few parts will make up most of our usage, but the parts with low usage will make up most of our service parts inventory. *(True)*

61. When deciding where to stock service parts, you want the minimum number of stocking locations that allow you to meet the service terms you sold your customers. *(True)*

62. It is best to co-locate service part inventory at the same site where product assembly occurs. *(False, on a global basis this is not even possible, plus what happens when the product is no longer being sold)*

63. Service part fill rate performance is impacted by product diagnostic capability, part availability, warehouse delay and shipment delay. *(True)*

64. Companies need to strive for 100% fill rate of service parts. *(False, companies could not afford the inventory required. They must have a defined plan on how they will expedite out of stock situations)*

65. We can always ask the customer to dispose of used service parts. *(False, some parts have environmental disposition rules)*

66. In setting up a strip/salvage operation, you must consider how you will dispose of chemicals. *(True)*

67. During product design, the design team needs to agree on what will be an acceptable level of service. *(True)*
68. The service engineer, as the subject matter expert, is the best person to write and publish knowledge articles. *(False, the service engineer is an expert on the product, and typically not an expert on proper communicating to an audience, they typically have little interest in proper usage of trademarks, and are not proficient at establishing proper meta data required to manage the knowledgebase and facilitate search)*
69. A key principle in performing data analytics is asking the question "what's different". *(True)*
70. Service needs to be profitable for each and every customer serviced. *(False, for some companies service and consumables need to be profitable and not service alone. Plus there is an insurance aspect on the sale of service agreements, particularly for high cost parts)*
71. Effective customer profitability analytics allows drill down by customer, by geography, and by product. *(True)*
72. Sales and marketing, service operations, and product engineering will each find value in analyzing customer profitability. *(True)*
73. Ranking reports are effective tools to allow us to separate high performing and low performing populations to better understand causes of customer service. *(True)*
74. Service organizations can embrace statistical process control. *(True)*
75. Contract administration is how we administer our service contracts, and therefore our service entitlements. *(True)*
76. Evergreen service agreements have a defined effective and expiration dates. Traditional service agreements have a

defined effective date, but remain in place until the customer provides advance notice to cancel. *(False, it would have been true if the words traditional and evergreen were reversed in the statement)*

77. Proper "change management", especially by leadership, will determine whether an improvement project is successful. *(True)*

78. Globalizing service processes has minimum requirements for change management. *(False, change management is "huge" in any initiative to globalize service processes)*

79. For service, R&D is the continual renewal and improvement in our service processes and systems. *(True)*

80. Service systems must be designed to easily interconnect with our customer's, partner's and supplier's systems. *(True)*

Summary

The marketplace is very competitive. Every day, new and existing companies want to displace your company. Simply stated, how well you provide your customers service is one option to allow you a competitive advantage and to survive.

Invariably you will introduce a new product which does not "wow" the marketplace or for which there are reliability issues. Until it can be corrected, you are highly vulnerable in the marketplace and will need to depend on service to bail you out. You will need to provide great service to keep your customers.

My intent with this book was to educate students and others about what is required for great service. I suspect this book was an eye opening experience for most of you, since you had no idea what was required to have a successful service experience for your customers.

Hopefully some of you may even decide that customer service is a career you want to pursue. There are many career opportunities. These include:

- Incident handling team
- Response center engineers
- Service depot technicians
- On-site service technicians
- Knowledge and education specialists
- Professional service specialists
- Service engineers
- Service part planning specialists

- o Part logistic personnel
- o Contract administrators
- o Service leadership

With your new knowledge, go forward and use service as a competitive weapon as you bring products to the marketplace and make career choices about your future.

Good luck.

John L. Bustard

April, 2015

www.ingramcontent.com/pod-product-compliance
Lightning Source LLC
Chambersburg PA
CBHW051921170526
45168CB00001B/490